ADVICE TO MY YOUNGER ME

ADVICE TO MY YOUNGER ME

Career Lessons from 100 Successful Women

SARA HOLTZ

LIONCREST
PUBLISHING

Hardcover ISBN: 978-1-5445-2510-5
Paperback ISBN: 978-1-5445-2509-9
eBook ISBN: 978-1-5445-2508-2

To Ted and Billy—living proof that the children of working mothers grow into wonderful adults.

Contents

Introduction

Y ou're smart, talented, and ambitious. You want to achieve your highest potential in your career. You want to be financially rewarded for your contributions. You want to be challenged by and respected for your work. You want to do work you enjoy, and which has a positive impact. You want to have the freedom that comes with being economically self-sufficient. You want to have a rich life, filled with friends, family, and interesting experiences. In other words, you want to have a successful career.

I want that for you too.

Sadly, however, today's workplace is not a level playing field for women like you. There is explicit and implicit bias against women. Men out-earn women and get more promotions. Despite the business case for the positive impact of having women in leadership, the C-suite is still largely a male domain. The increase in the number of women in executive roles has been glacially slow.

What's a smart, talented, and career-focused woman like you to do? Wait for CEOs to wake up and increase the number of women on their leadership teams? Wait for managers to actively support the careers of the women they supervise? Wait for diversity and inclusion initiatives to produce the results they advocate?

I don't think so.

You need to take your career success into your own hands. But figuring out how to get from where you are today to where you want to be can be unclear and fraught with difficult choices. There are too few mentors to help you navigate the sometimes-confusing workplace.

I want this book, and its accumulated wisdom of hundreds of successful women, to be that mentor for you. I want women who have "been there, learned this" to share with you what they wish they had known when they were where you are in your career.

Far too often in my career as a business lawyer and a C-suite executive at Fortune 500 companies, I was faced with challenges I didn't know how to deal with. How could I get credit for what I accomplished without coming off as a braggart? What could I do when I was repeatedly interrupted by male colleagues? How long of a maternity leave could I take and still maintain my reputation as a committed professional? I felt like I had no one I could turn to for advice on these tricky issues because I had few female peers and even fewer women more senior than me.

When I left the corporate workplace after twenty years, I vowed that I would help make the workplace a less challenging, more fulfilling place for the women who came after me. I did this for twenty years by coaching and training thousands of women lawyers to help them get more clients. Later, I did it by producing and hosting the *Advice to My Younger Me* podcast, where I interviewed over 125 successful women about the career advice they would give to their younger selves. Those women ranged in age from their early thirties to their late seventies. They are CEOs, media, advertising, and tech executives, partners in law firms and management consulting firms, and experts on diversity and inclusion, negotiation, and the impostor syndrome.

In this book, I've distilled the accumulated wisdom of the guests on my *Advice to My Younger Me* podcast, the thousands of women I have coached, and my own experience, into a nine-step roadmap of how to achieve the career success you want and deserve.

The steps are a mixture of practical, actionable advice, inspiration, and a bit of tough love.

They are:

1. Be the architect of your career
2. Do your Right Work
3. Take smart risks
4. Say no
5. Invest in relationships
6. Ask for help
7. Be visible
8. Get feedback
9. Stay in the workplace

Each chapter of this book explores one of these topics in depth, with real-life stories and advice from women who have been where you are now. (Throughout the book, I have changed client names out of respect for their privacy. Anytime you see only a first name, the name has been changed, but the story is real.)

This is a book not just to be read but also to be put into action. Because I am a coach at heart, at the end of each chapter there are "coaching assignments": concrete actions to take to implement the advice contained in that chapter.

Often these assignments call upon you to reflect about your experiences. Sometimes the coaching assignments ask you to turn your insights into action. These are "baby steps" that will help you implement the chapter's advice. Please don't be overwhelmed by what these coaching assignments ask you to do. Take one small step at a time. Over time, these small actions will make a significant difference in your career success. Please don't skip over these coaching assignments. They are where the real benefit of reading this book will be manifested.

When you do these assignments, block out time on your calendar to do them. Honor that time as if it were an important commitment (because it is!). Buy a journal to write down your thoughts. Writing provides clarity and tells your brain: this is important; pay attention. Go someplace where you won't be interrupted. Leave your phone behind.

Before we begin this journey together, I have two things I want to acknowledge. I am conscious that this book is written for the subset of women who have been privileged to have gotten a good education and are therefore in a position to have a well-paid, professional job and to aspire to even a more successful one. Also, I am well aware that women of color and LGBTQIA+ women face especially daunting challenges (see, for example, 2017–2020 Women in the Workplace studies conducted by McKinsey and LeanIn.Org[1]) and that I am ill-equipped to provide nuanced advice on those specific challenges. Yet, my hope is that all readers will find some helpful and career-building advice in this book.

My sincere wish for you is that, fortified with the hard-earned wisdom shared in the following pages, you will boldly step into your career and succeed beyond your wildest dreams.

So, let's get started.

CHAPTER 1

Be the Architect
of Your Career

When I was in my late thirties, in the late 1980s, I was a Vice-President at a Fortune 500 company. At that time, there were very few women at that level in any major company. The head of HR at my company organized a presentation by the company's four most senior women, of which I was one, to speak to the more junior women about our careers. I walked into a room full of smart, ambitious, and attentive women, dressed in suits and high heels. They were there eager to learn our "secrets" to career success.

When it came time for me to speak about my career, I described it as a sort of haphazard "I did good work, and one thing led to another" journey. No vision, no plan, no ownership, no risks. Just a mixture of smarts, head-down hard work, and luck.

Looking back, I am appalled at the picture I chose to paint that day. It was a message of such passivity. I was uncomfortable acknowledging my ambition (that would have been so distasteful!) and the intentionality with which I had navigated my career (that would have seemed so calculating!). Somehow, it seemed preferable to project the image of someone who had gotten where I was because of a combination of long hours and good fortune.

But the truth was, I had been ambitious. I had strategically built and leveraged my network. I had been politically savvy in dealing with the organizations in which I worked. I had taken some significant risks. In short, I had taken responsibility for how my career progressed.

If I could rewind the clock and deliver that presentation again, I would say, "It's your career. How it unfolds is your responsibility. No one will care about your career as much as you should. Be intentional and craft the career that you want."

TAKE CHARGE OF YOUR CAREER

Many women abdicate ownership of their careers. They ride the wave of what is happening and wait for opportunities to come along. Shellye Archambeau, former tech CEO, public company board member and author of *Unapologetically Ambitious: Take Risks, Break Barriers and Create Success on Your Own Terms*, shared this analogy:

> You would never spend thousands of dollars for an airline ticket, put your dog in the kennel, pack your bags, get to the airport, board the plane, and then ask

the pilot, "So where are we going?" But we do that all the time with our careers. We spend tens, if not hundreds of thousands, of dollars on our education, on training, on coaches, on conferences, on all these things to help us, and then we abdicate control of our career.

This passive attitude is like being in the passenger seat, rather than the driver's seat, of your career. Being in the passenger seat is certainly more comfortable, but it may not take you where you want to go.

One of my clients, Deanna, always wanted to be a teacher. But when she went to sign up for a major in education, she was told that there were only a limited number of spots available, and male students were being given preference because of the shortage of male elementary school teachers. She accepted that explanation and picked English as her major. After college, she found a job as a legal secretary, was quickly promoted to being a paralegal, and ultimately became a lawyer. She had a successful big-firm legal career, made a lot of money, and garnered a lot of respect. But to this day, she wishes that she hadn't let herself be so easily talked out of getting her teaching degree. Despite all the benefits that came with being a lawyer (including a large salary), she feels that being a teacher would have been a more satisfying and meaningful career.

Taking ownership of how your career unfolds is key to having the career you dream of. As Dana Look-Arimoto, executive coach and author of *Stop Settling, Settle Smart:*

Rethinking Work–Life Balance, Redesign Your Busy Life, urges, "Make your career choices by design, not default."

You don't need someone else's permission to tell you that you are ready for that stretch assignment or promotion. You can ask for it. You don't need someone else to tell others about your stellar work. You can make your accomplishments visible. You don't need to wait for someone to give you a raise. You can make the case that you deserve it. You don't need to hope that when the time comes to look for a new job, you'll know the right people to alert you to opportunities. You can intentionally build a network to support your career goals. You can be the architect of your career.

DEFINE YOUR VERSION OF SUCCESS

The first step in being the architect of your career is to decide what career success looks like for you. For example:

- Do you want to reach the C-suite in a big company? Or is your ultimate goal to be a founder of a start-up?
- What role does money play in your version of success?
- Do you want a job that has a lot of variety or is predictability important?
- Do you want a career that is compatible with being home for dinner every night? Or do you want a job that sends you flying all over the world working in different time zones and cultures?

- Is status or recognition important to you? Or do you measure success in terms of the impact on those you serve?
- Do you want a job that provides a secure paycheck? Or are you willing to take greater risks in the hope of greater rewards?
- Do you want to work as a member of a team or as an individual contributor?
- Is the culture of the company or its location important to you? Or will you accept any position that gives you the right opportunities?

The questions can go on and on.

Too often, when we talk about success, we focus only on money and titles, but as the above list makes clear, there are many more aspects to work that make you excited to get out of bed each day to go to work. Defining success as ascending to the C-suite of a company, making partner at a consulting firm, or becoming department head of your medical specialty may be what will make you happy. Making lots of money is a worthy goal if that is what is important to you. But the important thing is that your version of success be *your* version of success.

TUNE OUT OTHER VOICES

Developing a vision of what your successful career looks like seems like it would be relatively easy, but in my experience, it's not. Since you were very young, you have been receiving messages about what career you should pursue. Your parents, teachers, friends, co-workers, bosses, and even the media all have opinions about what a bright woman like you should want. Your father tells you that the best job for you is as an accountant in a big accounting firm, with a stable income, an excellent 401(k), and regular promotions. Your mother says that being a lawyer is too demanding a job to combine with motherhood. Your roommate cautions you that her sister, who works in tech, hates it because it's such a boy's club. The articles you read tell you that you should want to be the CEO of a Fortune 500 company or the founder of a tech start-up. Your favorite TV show paints a picture of the unmarried female doctor as miserable and lonely.

A study by KPMG, a global tax, audit, and advisory services firm, asked 3,000 college-aged and professional women what messages they received growing up.[2] The four most common answers were:

- Be nice to others (86 percent)
- Be a good student (86 percent)
- Be respectful of authority figures or elders (85 percent)
- Be helpful (77 percent)

At the bottom of the list?

- Share your point of view (34 percent)
- Be a good leader (44 percent)

Messages like these are certainly not consistent with being a successful business executive!

Others' opinions about what career you should pursue can be useful data. As Eileen McDargh, executive coach, Founder and CEO of the Resiliency Group and author of *Burnout to Breakthrough: Building Resilience to Refuel, Recharge, and Reclaim What Matters*, says, "Sometimes people see things in you that you don't see in yourself." But others' views should not limit or define your career decisions.

The well-intentioned advice from others may be right in the abstract, but it may not be right for you. They don't know what your big, unspoken dreams are. They don't know what excites you and what you find boring. They don't know what you are doing when time flies and what you are doing when you can't stop watching the clock. And most importantly, they don't have to live with the consequences of the decisions you make.

The career of one of my podcast guests, Melanie Vetter, illustrates the power of these early messages to lead to a less-than-satisfying career. Melanie was the child of immigrant parents who believed that the path to financial security and a happy life was by becoming a prestigious professional. As a child, she dreamed of being a chef, an art historian, or a theatrical make-up artist (notice the theme of creativity). But she followed her parents' urgings and went to Harvard Law School. Unsurprisingly, while she was successful as a lawyer, she did not find the work fulfilling. After many twists and turns in her career, she figured out what she really wanted to do was use her creative talents to help people find a deep connection with themselves and others through writing. She invented the job of "transformational writing coach." She founded Wellfleet Circle, where she teaches people how to get clarity around their values and purpose through journaling.

I had a client, Pauline, who was a brilliant litigator, consistently ranked among the best of the best—smart, strategic, no-nonsense. But she didn't start out her career as a lawyer. She started out as a social worker. The first time she told me this, I literally burst out laughing. Her strong personality and brilliant analytical skills didn't seem like a good match for being a social worker.

When I asked why she had thought that being a social worker was a good idea, she said that when she was in college, she didn't have a clear picture of what a woman with her talents could do. She had a college professor who told her he thought she would make a great social worker. Here was this older, experienced professor who saw a clear career path for her. She chose to follow his advice.

Despite all the well-intentioned advice you get from others, only you can make the choice about the right career path for you. Spend some time identifying the messages you've received about the career you should pursue and question whether those narratives serve you well now. Tune out those voices that do not serve you well and develop your own picture of what success means for you.

DRAW ON YOUR DEFINITION OF SUCCESS

Your definition of success provides you with a framework to fashion your short- and long-term goals. You can use it to develop the "big picture" goals that you hope to accomplish over the next few years, such as getting promoted to director, getting your real estate license, or polishing your communication skills. You can then use those goals to develop your monthly or quarterly goals, such as read a book on becoming a better manager, research on-line real estate license courses, or participate in Toastmasters.

Your definition of success can also serve as a benchmark as you measure your progress towards your goals. It's tempting to feel unsuccessful when you hear that your roommate from college has just been promoted to Vice-President, and you are still a Manager. When your sister buys a house, it can make you feel like a failure if you only have $2,000 in your savings account. But if your definition of success has nothing to do with titles or home ownership, there's no reason to feel diminished by their accomplishments.

Clarity around your definition of success can also help you make tough decisions—like whether to move across the country for a big promotion, leave your boring but well-paying job for the adventure of a start-up, or go back to school to get your PhD in robotics.

Shortly after I left my corporate job as General Counsel at a Fortune 500 company in California, I got a phone call from a headhunter about a job in a small city on the East

Coast. It paid twice what I'd been making at my old job. Initially, I was tempted to interview for the job. After all, it was so much money!

But I'd recently worked with a career coach to help me figure out what my next career move should be. After weeks of conversation and much thought, I'd come up with my personal definition of career success at that point in my life. It included:

- Spending most of my day doing what I considered my "Right Work" (we'll address Right Work in Chapter 2)
- Managing as few people as possible
- Making enough money to have a comfortable lifestyle and save for my children's college education and my retirement
- Leveraging what I'd already accomplished
- Having the flexibility to be actively involved in parenting my two young sons
- Traveling overnight on business no more than once a month
- Working with other talented women
- Being respected for the work I did
- Living in a place I loved
- Having a positive impact on the lives of others

When I reviewed my definition of success, I realized that no matter how much money was involved in this new job, it met few of my criteria. I would be spending a lot of time away from home on business travel, and I wouldn't have flexibility in where and when I did my work. I'm a big city girl and doubted I would adapt well to living in a small town, far away from family and friends.

I can't say it was easy, but I called the headhunter back and said I wasn't interested in the position. There were plenty of people who thought I was crazy. But because I had such clarity around what success meant to me, I was comfortable with the decision, and I've never regretted it.

DON'T WORRY IF YOU DON'T KNOW WHAT YOU WANT

What if you don't have a crystal-clear definition of your version of success? Take a deep breath and don't beat yourself up. I know a woman who knew exactly what she wanted to do since she was four years old. She wanted to be a doctor, have two children, and live in New York City. And that's exactly what she did. But I have known many more women who were not sure what they wanted to do when they were thirty. Yet, all of them have wound up with successful careers.

A key tenet of one of my favorite career-planning resources, the book *Designing Your Life: How to Build a Well-Lived, Joyful Life* by Bill Burnett and Dave Evans, is that there is no one, best career. Many jobs would bring you satisfaction, draw on your strengths and interests, and pay you well. Feeling that you need to figure out the "perfect career" may get in the way of finding a very good one.

Oftentimes you need experience in the real world to figure out what you do and don't want out of your career. It may be that, only by working in a male-dominated, competitive organization, you come to realize that it's important to you to work in a collaborative environment. Or you may discover from a calendar full of business trips that business travel is exhausting and not nearly as glamourous as you thought.

Further, your definition of success will likely evolve over time, as your opportunities, family situation, and experiences change. At the outset of my career, I was all about titles and recognition. I wanted to be seen as a trailblazer. I wanted validating promotions and a salary that indicated that my contributions were being valued. Once I had children, my definition of success changed dramatically. Success was a "balanced" life of meaningful work that drew on my strengths, a flexible schedule so that I could spend time with my family, and enough money for a comfortable lifestyle. After my kids were launched in their own careers, my definition of career success once again morphed to being laser-focused on helping younger women succeed in the workplace.

EMBRACE THE IDEA OF MULTIPLE CAREERS

I often say that "Careers are long but rarely linear." It's unlikely that your career will be "one and done." Try as you might, you can't predict today the path your life will take as your career unfolds. You may go to graduate school thinking you know the career you want to pursue. You may be successful at it, only to discover later that you want to do work more aligned with your strengths and interests. You may follow the love of your life to a new city and find it hard to get a job in your current field, so you make a pivot to a new role. You may have kids and discover your super-demanding job no longer works for you, so you look for a career with more flexibility. You may find it's too hard to make a living doing the job you thought you would love, so you have to look for one that pays better. (By the way, all of those things happened to me!)

Former lawyer, Brenda Bernstein, says the best piece of career advice she ever received was that people have an average of three careers in their lives. "It was so helpful to learn that shifting careers was a normal thing that a lot of people do. It allowed me, after ten years as a lawyer, to give myself permission to embark on an entirely different career." She has since founded the Essay Expert, a company that helps executives write stellar resumes and LinkedIn profiles.

Shifting careers—sometimes dramatically—was a common theme among the women I interviewed. Nora McInerny went from being an advertising copywriter to an author and podcast host. Kelly Hoey started out as a corporate lawyer and is now a renowned expert on networking. Shasta Nelson started out as a minister and ended up founding a company supporting women's friendships.

Been There, Learned This:
Careers Are Rarely Linear

Nancy Davis Kho, author of *The Thank-You Project: Cultivating Happiness One Letter of Gratitude at a Time*, who went from international product management, to being a writer, to returning to the corporate world in a business development role, gave this advice about what she calls "twisty" career paths:

You may think you're going to be doing the thing that you're doing right now for the rest of your life, and maybe you will. But if you start feeling pulled in another direction, don't panic. Listen to that voice.

I had two degrees in international management. In my twenties, you could never have convinced me that I was going to be anything other than an international Captain of the Universe. And then, as I was coming up to forty, based on nothing, I thought, *Wait a minute. I think I'm a writer.* So, I started taking some writing classes, and lo and behold, that's what I wound up doing.

I've seen this pattern with so many of my friends who start off on path A, and now they're on path B, or maybe even path C. Just give yourself grace and listen to what you're curious about. You may think that the stuff you learn in your first career would never apply to your second or third career, but it does. The things you learn travel along with you.

It's simply not realistic to think you can make a decision today that will withstand the passage of time, given cultural and technological changes that are sure to occur during your lifetime. The last job you have before you retire may not even exist today!

STAY AMBITIOUS

Women often are ambivalent about being (or at least being perceived as being) ambitious. But if you are going to have your best possible career, you need to get comfortable with being ambitious—and letting others know that you are.

Research shows that over the course of a career, women tend to lose their ambition. In one study conducted by the global management consulting firm, Bain & Company, women with MBAs who were in their first two years of working were asked whether they aspired to top management within their companies. "The women gave a resounding yes," said Julie Coffman, a Partner and Global Head of Diversity, Equity, and Inclusion practice at Bain. "The women both wanted it and felt confident it could happen. In fact, they had higher aspirations than their male peers." But that changed quickly. "By three years into their careers, women's aspirations and confidence in achieving top roles plummeted, down by 50–60 percent." Coffman continued. "By then, only 16 percent of women had top management aspirations."

The blame for this diminution in ambition is usually placed on women having children. But the Bain researchers examined the data to see if this was the cause. "It turns out that is not the case," Coffman continued. "Marital or parental status did not predict who aspired to top roles and who no longer did." A McKinsey/LeanIn Women in the Workplace study reported, "Women are not leaving their companies at higher rates than men, and very few [women] plan to leave the workforce to focus on family."[3] In fact, another Women in the Workplace study found that women with children were 15 percent more likely to aspire to being a top executive than women without children.[4]

According to the Bain study, three factors contributed to women's loss of ambition:[5]

- Not seeing a path to being successful in their companies
- Not having a manager that supported their success with training, mentorship, and stretch opportunities
- Not seeing other women in senior roles in the company

The takeaway: if you want to maintain your ambition (and you should), look to work in organizations in which there are women in senior roles and seek out bosses who are supportive of your career goals. If you find yourself in a job or in an organization that doesn't do that, consider moving on to one that does. If that's not possible, be aware that being in an organization without women at the top or without a boss who supports your career advancement can sap your ambition. Be cognizant of your need to consciously maintain your ambition, despite the dearth of successful women around you.

A loss of ambition may not only be attributable to an unsupportive company culture. Sometimes lessened ambition is the result of self-limiting thoughts. Valerie Young, author of *The Secret Thoughts of Successful Women: Why Capable People Suffer from the Impostor Syndrome and How to Thrive in Spite of It*, and an internationally recognized authority on the impostor syndrome, described an experience she had speaking to a large audience of professional women:

> A woman raised her hand and said she was "kind of thinking about" positioning herself for an executive role, but she was concerned that executives worked a lot of hours. She didn't want to do that.
>
> When I dug deeper, what was really behind her reluctance was she didn't think she could do the job. It was a confidence issue. She felt like an impostor.
>
> My advice to her: "Go for it. Go find out that you really can do it. You can always change your mind later. You can always step back. But it's harder to step up if you've lost your chance."

In my coaching practice, I often heard from women who didn't want to go for the "big job"—whether it was a partner in a law firm or an executive in a company. They would say, "I look at the women who are more senior than I am, and I don't want their lives. They talk about how stressed out they are and they always look sleep deprived." My advice paralleled Young's: "Go get the big job. See whether you can do it differently. Maybe the reason they look so sleep deprived is because they haven't made sleep a priority. Maybe they've defined the job in such a way that it is all-consuming, but it doesn't necessarily have to be done that way. Sometimes the more senior you are, the more flexibility you have in the way you do your work."

Challenge the reasons you may have for lessening your ambitions. See if they are based in fact or on unexamined assumptions about what's required to be successful in a senior position.

INVEST TIME AND MONEY IN YOUR CAREER

Over the years, I've noticed that women are often reluctant to invest their own time and money in their careers. They hesitate to spend their out-of-work hours learning critical business skills—like how to read a financial statement, or how to be an inclusive leader—that are beyond the scope of their current job, even though these skills would contribute to their professional growth. They hesitate to spend their money on career-enhancing investments, like dues for a professional organization or the cost of a workshop on time management. They reason that if their company won't foot the bill, why should they?

Robin Farmanfarmaian, author of *The Thought Leader Formula: Strategically Leverage Your Expertise to Drive*

Business & Career Goals, points out that most people have the mistaken assumption that when they finish their formal education, they can stop investing in their careers:

> They say, "Now that I have my college or graduate degree, I'm done paying for my education." You know what? Your career needs to be looked at as a business. There isn't a single successful business that doesn't spend money to support their business. Even if you work for a company, you've got to pay to learn things and you've got to have a marketing budget to market yourself.

I had a client, Elena, who worked in banking in New York City. As one of our coaching calls was ending, she told me she was about to head out to a long-anticipated lunch with a potential client. Casually, I said, "Don't forget to pick up the check."

A bit taken aback, she responded, "You know, lunch in New York is really expensive, and the company won't pay for it."

I responded, "You've worked really hard and waited months to get this lunch appointment. If the person you're meeting with leaves feeling even slightly put off by the fact that you didn't pay for lunch, you've lost somebody who's potentially a client, a mentor, or an important addition to your network. That's a risk you shouldn't take. You need to realize that sometimes you have to spend your own money as an investment in your career."

Don't be short-sighted about investing your time and money in your career. It's an investment that will pay off!

KEY TAKEAWAYS

Lewis Carroll wrote in *Alice in Wonderland*, "If you don't know where you are going, any road will take you there." The inverse is equally true. If you want to get somewhere in your career, however you define that "somewhere," you need to figure out which road you should travel. And then, you need to take responsibility for taking the steps necessary to get you where you want to go.

You need to be both good at your job and good at your career. The choices you make and the actions you take today—the way you nurture your network, the risks you take, and the help you ask for—will have important ramifications for your future success.

How to do those things successfully is what the rest of this book is about.

Coaching Assignments:

Put This Chapter into Action

1. **Reflect on the messages you received growing up about what your career aspirations should be.**

   Which of these messages serve you well when envisioning the career of your dreams? Which of these messages don't?

   Write down a list of the unhelpful messages. Every time you find yourself reluctant to make a career-enhancing move, think about whether one of those unhelpful messages is getting in the way of you taking that action. If so, challenge that thought to see if it is really true.

2. **Develop your definition of success.**

   Carve out time to do some deep work on defining what your version of a successful career looks like. Refer to some of the questions raised on page 4–5. You can probably come up with even more that are relevant to you.

Write down what you come up with. Don't worry if your definition isn't perfect. You can revise it as you continue to think about it more.

3. **Stay ambitious.**

   Commit in writing to doing one thing in the next year that will move your career forward. It should be big enough to scare you a little—like asking for a raise or a promotion, seeking a stretch assignment, or enlisting a mentor.

4. **Set up a budget for career investments.**

   Set aside money that you will spend on building your skills or your network. What professional organization could you join and actively participate in? Who could you take out to lunch to ask for career advice? What professional conference could you attend to inspire you? Then spend that money investing in your career.

CHAPTER 2

Do Your Right Work

A number of years ago, I received the prestigious Margaret Brent Women Lawyers of Achievement Award from the American Bar Association. Along with the award came the opportunity (or, some would no doubt say, the curse) of giving a speech to a room filled with hundreds of people. On the morning of the award, my younger son, Billy, asked me if I was nervous. I replied truthfully that I wasn't. He found that surprising, since he, along with many other people, would have found speaking in front of a large audience anxiety-producing. But speaking in front of groups is my Right Work. I am energized when I do it and consistently get positive feedback about my presentations. Silly as it may seem, I didn't always realize that other people didn't find public speaking as much fun as I do.

WHAT IS "RIGHT WORK"?

Each of us has what I call your Right Work. Some people call it your strengths, your gifts, your talents, your unique abilities, or your superpowers—or simply what you are really good at. It's work that draws on your innate abilities. It's work that seems relatively easy for you to do and that's deeply satisfying when you do it. It's what you are doing when you produce your best results or have the most significant impact. It's those activities for which you have superior skills and that you love doing. It's the work that lights you up.

Your Right Work might be sensing what others are feeling, which enables you to reach consensus among diverse stakeholders. It might be persuading others to agree to your proposal because you communicate clearly and concisely. Your Right Work might be helping a team that is drowning in data see the big picture. It could be being able to walk into a room full of strangers and start a conversation with anyone there.

Your Right Work is not a specific job category like being an emergency room doctor, a marketing executive, or a purchasing manager. It is the talents you bring to your job. You can do your Right Work in many different types of jobs. For example, if your Right Work is being a dynamic team leader, you could be a manager at a pharmaceutical company, the director of a political campaign, or an officer in the military. If your Right Work is being an empathetic listener, you could be a primary care physician, a high school counselor, or a journalist. If your Right Work is being a stellar networker, you could be a venture capitalist, a real estate agent, or a fundraiser for a non-profit.

Taking the time to discover your Right Work is critical because your greatest opportunity for career success comes when you focus on and leverage your strengths. The Gallup organization has found that doing what you excel at makes you six times as likely to be engaged at work and more than three times as likely to be happy with your life.[6]

Anne Elkin, Vice-President for Human Resources at Qualcomm, says:

> When you are working in a place where you are leveraging your strengths versus trying to improve your weaknesses, you're much more successful. It's kind of like going with the tide. If you're working with your strengths, you are riding the tide, rather trying to force your way through it.

It also makes sense to focus on our strengths, since the truth is, we aren't very good at overcoming our weaknesses (despite the emphasis that is often placed on improving our weaknesses in performance reviews). Trying to "fix" our shortcomings—like not being detailed-oriented, not being good with numbers, or not thinking outside the box—is not likely to be very successful.

Elkin had me do an exercise to illustrate just how time-consuming and frustrating it can be to overcome our weaknesses. She had me sign my name ten times with my dominant hand (I'm right-handed). Then, she had me sign my name ten times with my non-dominant hand. Since I'm not ambidextrous, I found that signing with my right hand was easy, quick, and legible, while signing with my left hand was time-consuming, frustrating, and far less legible. My first try at the left-handed signature was basically scribble. By the tenth time, I'd managed to produce something legible—but just barely.

As this exercise shows, we can get better at things that are not our natural strengths, but it takes a lot of time and effort, and in the end, we don't get all that much better. We can move our performance from awful to mediocre, but we rarely get to great.

Whatever your strengths are, they can be the building blocks for a successful career, so it's important you identify your special talents and learn to leverage them.

IDENTIFY YOUR RIGHT WORK

Over the years, I've found that many people struggle to identify their Right Work. Often, they are oblivious to their strengths because they come so easily to them. We sometimes think that for something to be valuable, it has to be difficult. If dealing with demanding customers or being a great team contributor is your strength, you just assume everybody can do it.

But that's not true. Just because it is easy for you doesn't mean that it's not uniquely valuable. Some people lose their cool when dealing with a difficult customer, needlessly escalating the situation. Some people are horrible team members, preferring to work alone. Some people instinctively make crisp presentations, while others struggle to get to the main point.

Jenny Blake, a change strategy consultant and author of *Pivot: The Only Move That Matters Is Your Next One,* gave this example of being oblivious to her own gifts:

> I have an immaculately color-coded bookshelf that I've worked on for three years. When people come over, they notice it. I realized only slowly, and with lots of feedback from others, that creating order out of chaos was a strength of mine. When I shared what I considered to be this amazing insight with a friend, she said, "Oh, that's so obvious. Look at your bookshelf. That says it all."

Blake's gift of making order out of chaos is not limited to having a color-coded bookshelf. It's something she does in her job helping people navigate career change. For many people, deciding how to look for a new job is fraught with uncertainty and anxiety. But to Blake, it is a clearly defined, step-by-step, replicable process. She spells the process out clearly in her book, and she uses it to coach those in transition.

While it can be challenging to identify your Right Work, there are several strategies you can use.

Reflect on Your Work Experiences

Discovering your Right Work can be as simple (or as hard) as being curious and reflecting on your work and life experiences. Recall when you were most engaged in a task at work and notice when you do your best work. Pay attention to when you are bored, struggle, or produce sub-optimal results. Hone in on the things that come naturally to you but are challenging for others. Keep a running list of things that are so innate that, metaphorically, you feel like you could do them with your eyes closed.

My Right Work includes:

- Asking thought-provoking questions and really listening to the answers
- Researching and synthesizing information
- Communicating in a way that people find actionable
- Building strong one-on-one relationships
- Helping successful people become more successful

I came up with this list by reflecting on the common elements in jobs I enjoyed and at which I excelled.

To identify your Right Work, it can be helpful to start by focusing on a typical workweek at your current job. Reflect on questions like these:

- What parts of your job come easily to you?
  - Developing a budget?
  - Learning a new software program?

- Engaging with customers?
- Which aspects of your work energize you?
  - Leading a team?
  - Negotiating with vendors?
  - Synthesizing complicated information?
- What parts of a project are you excited to volunteer for?
  - Developing the timeline?
  - Serving on a committee?
  - Writing the report?
- When are you "in the zone"?
  - Researching?
  - Brainstorming?
  - Presenting?
- What is it that you bring to a project that has the most significant impact on its success?
  - Conflict management?
  - Project planning?
  - Creative ideas?

Molly Beck, Founder and CEO of Messy.fm, a company that provides podcasting resources for organizations, and author of *Reach Out: The Simple Strategy You Need to Expand Your Network and Increase Your Influence*, suggests another, simple approach to discovering your Right Work. Think about your current and previous jobs. Write down what you loved and what you hated about each one. What are the common themes that emerge? Since we tend to like things we are good at and dislike things that we don't do so well, this can be a helpful way to articulate your strengths.

Think about What You Did as a Child

It can be helpful to look back at the things you were good at and enjoyed doing when you were a kid. How did you spend your free time? What do you remember being praised for? Your Right Work is often hard-wired from when you were young.

I recently came across a photograph that illustrates just how hard-wired my presentation skills are. In the picture, I am about four years old. I have set up a circle of small chairs, and there is a doll sitting in each one. I am standing in front of them, holding a book, and "reading" to them. As the photograph made clear, as a little girl, when I played with dolls, I didn't change their clothes or style their hair. Instead, I would pretend to be their teacher at the front of the room.

When my oldest son, Ted, was in second grade, he was assigned a math worksheet to complete. The worksheet called for him to do a math word problem: if there were two ducks and then three more ducks joined them, how many ducks in total would there be? He was told to do the calculation and then to draw a picture illustrating the answer.

When his worksheet was returned, his teacher had written at the top, "Unfortunately, the answer is wrong. However, these are the best pictures of ducks I have ever seen a seven-year-old draw!"

Even at seven years old, his Right Work was apparent. His Right Work does not involve computation skills but rather visual communication. Luckily for him, today he spends most of his day doing his Right Work as an editor and director of digital media.

Get Input from Others

Because we are often blind to what we do well, it's valuable to get input from others. In articulating your Right Work, it can be helpful to ask others for their views on what you do well. Awkward as it may feel, go to someone who you have worked with a lot and ask them what they see as your talents. Ask:

- What do you see as my strengths?
- What do I do easily that others find more difficult?
- When we have worked together, where have I added the most value?

I know this can feel uncomfortable because it seems like you are fishing for compliments. Or you may be afraid of what you may hear. But through the years, I have encouraged my clients to "just do it." Despite their initial reluctance, not a single person has regretted having done it! The feedback they got was invaluable in helping them see their Right Work more clearly.

When someone says, "Wow, you really handled that situation well," take note. Think about the positive feedback you got in your last performance review. Notice the things that people ask for your input on. All of these things point to what your Right Work may be.

Finally, there's a wealth of assessment tools that can provide you with another window into your natural gifts. Tools like StrengthsFinder, Myers-Briggs, Kolbe, and DISC can be additional data points to help you understand what you do best.

By paying attention to all of these various inputs, your Right Work should become increasingly apparent to you. Once you are able to recognize and articulate your Right Work, you will be in a position to identify situations where you can leverage it to be happier and more successful. It can allow you to figure out if a potential job will be a good match and help you avoid nightmare "opportunities."

IDENTIFY YOUR "RIGHT WORK ENVIRONMENT"

Finding your Right Work is not just about finding a job that leverages your talents. It is also about finding the Right Work Environment in which you can do your best work and thrive. Even if you have a job doing your Right Work, if the environment is wrong, you may wind up unhappy.

Realizing which work environment matches your personality and temperament can have a dramatic impact on your job performance and career satisfaction. You just need to figure out what that environment is.

Once again, it's a matter of paying attention, this time to your reactions to your environment. Do high-pressure situations make you anxious, or do they exhilarate you? Do you like stability or variety? Do you love a day with lots of meetings and interactions with co-workers, or are you delighted to have a three-hour block of time to work on a project without interruption?

Many years ago, I was on an airplane sitting next to this cute guy who was an FBI agent. By way of striking up a conversation, he asked me, "So, what's your day like?"

At the time, I was a lawyer working for a large company. I described my day:

> I have an hour-long commute to work on public transportation. I arrive at work at 8:30 a.m. I go to my office in a high-rise building. I sit at my desk in my office, which has a beautiful view, with the door slightly ajar. I write and rewrite memos and legal documents. I talk on the phone a lot. Sometimes clients come to my office to talk through a legal issue. Sometimes I go a few floors down to see them. I usually have lunch with my co-workers, but sometimes I do errands during my lunch break. I leave the office about 6:00 p.m. I read the newspaper or a book on my commute home. Then, maybe I have dinner with a friend, or watch TV, or read a book before I fall into bed, exhausted, at about 10:00 p.m.

He replied, somewhat incredulously, "You sit at a desk all day? You basically do the same thing, day in and day out? Oh my god, that would kill me."

A bit taken aback, I asked, "So, what's your day like?"

He responded:

> Hmm, you know, every day it's different. Some days I show up at my office about 9:00 a.m. to do paperwork. Some days I'm on a stakeout starting at midnight. Sometimes it's excruciatingly boring just waiting around for someone to show up, and sometimes it's exhilarating, like breaking down a door, going into a house with guns drawn, and not knowing what to expect there. Some days I wear a suit and tie, and some days I wear jeans. No two days are the same.

As he was describing his days, my eyes grew wide. "Well, that job would kill *me!*"

On a slightly less dramatic note, I have friends who are trial lawyers. There's a lot of conflict in their workday. They are often arguing with opposing counsel. They lead a life with a constantly changing calendar. They have a deposition scheduled 2,000 miles away on Wednesday, but on Tuesday night, it gets cancelled. They block off two months on their calendars for an upcoming trial, and then, a week before the trial, the case gets settled, and their calendar is now empty.

I couldn't do that job either. I need a job that is relatively predictable. I need to be able to schedule my life. I need to be interacting with people regularly, but I also need to be able to close my door and do uninterrupted work for sustained periods of time. The less drama, the less conflict, the better, as far as I am concerned.

Once you identify your Right Work Environment, sometimes you can make small tweaks to align your current work environment with your best workstyle—having a meeting-free morning so you can do concentrated work, taking a phone call while going for a walk so you can get a break from sitting at a desk, or establishing an in-person team check-in every morning to satisfy your need for human interaction. But sometimes, working in your Right Work Environment requires finding a new job setting.

Been There, Learned This: The "Wrong Work Environment" Can Make You Miserable

Sometimes the gulf between how you do your best work and your current work environment is just too great to be sustainable. Morra Aarons-Mele, author of *Hiding in the Bathroom: An Introvert's Roadmap to Getting Out There (When You'd Rather Stay Home)*, shared this poignant story with me about how she struggled at work when she was in what she calls a "bad space, place, and pace":

> I would get these jobs, and I would be so unhappy. I thought I was in the wrong career. I would have panic attacks. I would feel depressed. I would cry in the bathroom. I couldn't figure out why I was so miserable. I felt like something was wrong with me. Often, I would just quit.

It was only after a process of quitting many jobs that I realized it wasn't the work that I did that was making me so unhappy; it was how I was doing it. I was not fit to show up in a high-pressure, high-paced, overstimulating office environment every day. I just couldn't do it.

How your work environment feels to you matters. Once I left the corporate world and started my own company, where I could design my workday and work environment, I was much happier and more successful.

IDENTIFY YOUR "WRONG WORK"

Just as important as knowing what your Right Work is, is knowing what your Wrong Work is.

Few of us set out to do work we don't like and which we aren't particularly good at, but this happens more often than you might imagine. For example, good individual performers often get promoted into management roles, without regard to whether they are likely to be good at or enjoy managing people. Or your boss wants to get something off her plate, so she assigns it to you, regardless of whether it is a strength of yours.

But spending a lot of time doing your Wrong Work can have a negative impact on your confidence, and it can result in you producing sub-par work. Your best self is definitely not showing up when you are spending much of your day doing your Wrong Work.

Sometimes figuring out your Wrong Work is easy; it's simply the opposite of your Right Work. If working alone on a research-intensive project is your Right Work, then working on a team with constant brainstorming is probably your Wrong Work. If your talents lie in seeing the big picture, work that requires being detail-oriented is probably your Wrong Work. If you are independent and creative, work that requires adherence to routine processes is probably your Wrong Work.

But sometimes it's not that simple.

Don't Confuse Capabilities with Strengths

It's easy to confuse your Right Work with work that you are capable of doing. But those can be two very different things.

As I was contemplating leaving my corporate job, I worked with a career coach to figure out what I should do next. In one of the exercises we did, I was given a large stack of cards, each with a skill on it. The skills were wide-ranging—ability to write computer code, speak in front of groups, manage a team, or edit a memo. The counselor told me to divide the cards into two piles: things I could do and things I couldn't. Write code went into one pile (guess which one); manage a team into another. Then she told me to go through the collection of cards of those things I could do and sort them into two more piles: things I wanted to do in my next job and those I didn't. I stared at her blankly. It had never occurred to me that I could be capable of doing something (like, in my case, managing a team) and not want to do it (managing teams was often frustrating for me).

After I realized that I didn't have to pursue a job that involved something that I could do, but really didn't want to do, a world of possibilities opened up. I didn't need to work in a large organization. I didn't need to manage a large staff. I could choose to work with a small team of self-starters in my own business. To this day, I think that insight was critical to the long-term success of my business. I was able to focus my energies on my Right Work—and not be drained by my Wrong Work.

Don't Be Blinded by What You Think You Should Be Good At

Sometimes our Wrong Work is something we think we should be good at, but we just aren't. As much as we might want something to be a strength of ours, it just isn't. When I was doing coaching, I was sometimes asked to coach people who were on the verge of getting fired. While I liked to think of myself as an all-around good coach, I discovered that I wasn't very good at turning sub-par performers into acceptable contributors. I rarely was able to get these people to a level their management wanted, and I was often frustrated working with them. As much as I wanted to think of myself as a good coach, I actually wasn't a good coach for everyone.

Eventually, I heeded the advice of Morra Aarons-Mele, author of *Hiding in the Bathroom*, "understand who you are and accept it." Once I did that, I turned down opportunities to coach struggling performers, and both my clients and I were more satisfied.

As an interesting aside, I might have realized that coaching sub-par performers was my Wrong Work earlier had I paid more attention to my StrengthsFinder results. It identifies one of my strengths as being a Maximizer, which is described as "seeking to transform something strong into something superb. Taking something from below average to slightly above average is, in your opinion, not very rewarding."

DOING MORE OF YOUR RIGHT WORK

Regrettably, few people get to spend all their time in their ideal work environment, doing things that energize them and at which they excel. Early in your career, it can be especially hard to spend the majority of your day doing your Right Work. Just because you know what your Right Work is doesn't mean that your job description calls for it or your boss will let you do it. Maybe you are really good at creating engaging PowerPoint presentations, but your job calls on you to interact with customers all day. Maybe your sweet spot is managing a project, but you are the most junior member on the team. Even when I ran my own business and could spend most of my day doing my Right Work (coaching one-on-one with high-achieving women professionals), I still needed to deal with the administrivia of running the business and the need to manage my small, high-performing staff, tasks which were definitely not my Right Work.

But even small changes in how much of your day is spent doing your Right Work can have a major impact on how much you enjoy your work. A study from the Mayo Clinic found that physicians who spend just 20 percent of their time doing "work they find most meaningful" are at dramatically lower risk for burnout.[7]

Without changing jobs, you can take baby steps to increase the amount of time you spend each day doing your Right Work. Perhaps you can tweak your job without needing anyone else's buy-in. For example, if one of your strengths is project planning, you could write a post-meeting summary about the action steps and deadlines that were agreed upon in the meeting, highlight any missing steps, and circulate it to the team.

Perhaps there's a project you could volunteer for that would capitalize on one of your strengths. For example, if you are working in sales and one of your strengths is written communication, you could volunteer to write a "best practices" white paper for your sales team on dealing with difficult-to-reach customers. Or, if one of your strengths is mentoring, you could cancel the Monday morning team check-in meeting that you chair and instead meet individually with each of your reports for fifteen minutes a week. The status updates could be handled on Slack instead of in the weekly meeting.

Negotiate to Do Your Right Work

If spending more time doing your Right Work requires the blessing of your manager, do as Carson Tate, executive coach and author of *Own it. Love It. Make It Work: How to Make Any Job Your Dream Job*, suggests: describe how using your strength on a project could help achieve a goal of your manager or the company. Demonstrate that leveraging your unique ability will mean a project can be completed faster, cheaper, more innovatively, or will better serve customers. They won't fire you for asking, and they may be delighted to have you suggest a better way to do your job.

As an in-house lawyer, I was sometimes involved in situations where company employees had potentially exposed the company to legal risk—by firing an employee without proper documentation about their poor performance, or by not anticipating risks in a leasing agreement. It occurred to me that a way to avoid these situations in the future would be to conduct "legal compliance" workshops on how to avoid these problems in advance. Doing these workshops drew on my strength of presenting before groups. When I proposed the idea to my boss, even though it is not how most lawyers do their jobs, he thought it was a great idea. It was a win-win. I got to do my Right Work, and the company achieved its goal of minimizing legal exposure.

Another option to consider is whether it's okay to not do your usual A+ job on tasks that don't draw on your strengths, thus freeing up time to do more of your Right Work. Women often feel they must bring their A game to everything they do. In reality, people often don't even notice what level of performance you are bringing to non-essential tasks.

I often advised my clients to consider doing a C+ job on non-essential tasks that were not their strengths. For example, my introverted clients were sometimes asked to attend large networking events. I'd suggest they go to the event but leave after thirty minutes. If they were asked to plan a summer intern picnic, and event planning was not a strength, I would urge them to delegate the task of planning it to someone else. The menu might not be what they would have chosen, but it was probably good enough.

Aiming for A+ results for your Wrong Work is going to be time consuming and unsatisfying. By lowering your standards for your Wrong Work, you have more time to do an A+ job on your Right Work. The results on those Right Work projects are more likely to be excellent, and you are likely to find them more fulfilling.

KEY TAKEAWAYS

Figuring out and then doing more of your Right Work is a way to supercharge your career. It's also a way to make sure that you find your career satisfying and meaningful to you. Take the time to identify your Right Work, your Wrong Work, and your Right and Wrong Work Environments, and then negotiate to do more of your Right Work in the Right Work Environment.

Coaching Assignments:

Put This Chapter into Action

1. **Pay close attention as you go through your workday for the next week.**

    When do you find your work energizing? When do you find it draining? When are you "in the zone"? When do you find yourself struggling to get through a task? What always drops to the bottom of your to-do list? What do you think you should be good at, but if you're honest, you really aren't? What are you capable of doing, but you're not all that excited about?

    Write down what you discover.

2. **Recall what people compliment you on.**

    What positive feedback have you gotten? What do people come to you for advice on? Go back and read your previous performance reviews. What are you consistently rated most highly on?

    Write down what other people see as your strengths.

3. **Reflect on what strengths were involved in your "big" successes.**

Think about when you made a big sale, organized a productive off-site meeting, improved the performance of a person you manage, or experienced another success. Which of your strengths were critical to these successes?

Write down your learnings in your notebook.

4. **Think about what you loved to do as a child.**

Did you like to play with Legos and build skyscrapers? Did you organize the neighborhood kids to sell lemonade? Did you make up stories to tell your younger brother? What can these early experiences tell you about what might be your Right Work?

Capture your thoughts in your notebook.

5. **Ask a few people for input on your strengths.**

You can use this book as the excuse for asking. Try something like:

I'm reading this book about career success. It says that focusing on your strengths can help you become more successful. It turns out that we're often blind to our own talents. The book suggests that I ask a few co-workers (or managers) who I really respect what they see as my strengths. Would you be willing to do that for me?

What are the common qualities that emerge? Summarize the feedback you get in your notebook.

6. **Focus on your work environment.**

What are the conditions in which you do your best work? Do you thrive on constant interaction or on long periods of concentrated work? Do you like working in an open office or in an empty conference room? Do you like working remotely or crave the interaction you get from working in the office?

Write down what you notice.

7. **Look for the patterns that emerge from all the information you've gathered.**

What have you discovered about your Right Work? Your Wrong Work? Your Right Work Environment? Your Wrong Work Environment?

Summarize what you've learned and keep it handy to review as you consider how you approach your job and how to evaluate new job opportunities.

8. **Consider how you could tweak your current job to utilize more of your strengths and restructure your work environment to make it better for you.**

   What tasks could you volunteer to do? What activities could you do less of, to a lower standard, or delegate to others? What changes could you make in your working environment to make it a better workplace for you? Which of these changes can you make on your own, and which do you need agreement from your boss or colleagues? What's your strategy for getting their buy-in?

   Choose one small thing you can do to increase the time you spend doing your Right Work and implement it this week. Evaluate whether it makes a difference in your energy or results. Next week, take another small action to do more of your Right Work. Continue doing this week after week.

9. **Be on the lookout for opportunities that draw on your strengths.**

   When you see them, volunteer to do them.

CHAPTER 3

Take Smart Risks

Someone looking at my career today might see it as a seamless progression from one job to the next. I was a lawyer. I moved from one legal position to another, getting more prestigious titles and making more money. I had an idea for a business, so I left lawyering to start a business. The business was a success. At the end of my career, I drew upon all the experience of my long career and launched a podcast providing career advice to younger women.

But the truth is much messier. My career was hardly linear. Many of the moves I made were risky, or at least they seemed so at the time. Some of the moves turned out to be utter failures.

When I graduated from law school, I didn't take the typical career path for Harvard Law School graduates—work at a large, prestigious law firm as an associate, do good work, become a partner, and stay there until retiring. I didn't even interview for those jobs, because I was afraid, despite my "with honors" diploma, I wouldn't get hired.

(Talk about being self-defeating!) Instead, I started out at a small, boutique law firm in Washington, D.C.

After a few years, I left the law firm to work in the federal government, thinking that would bolster my resume in government-focused law practice in Washington, D.C. I got promoted several times. But when the Administration changed from one party to another, I was "encouraged" to move on from the management role I was then in.

At the time, I was in love with a guy who was planning to move back to his hometown of San Francisco. I decided to follow him to a city where I had no professional connections, leaving behind the extensive network I had built in D.C. that presumably would have helped me get another job. (Yes, I moved to follow a boy, regardless of the impact it would have on my career. The boy part didn't work out so well.)

I thought it would be easy to find a job in the private sector in San Francisco, but that didn't turn out to be the case. I applied for a lot of law firm jobs and got a lot of polite rejection letters. It turned out that outside of Washington D.C., employers didn't value the skills I had developed in the government.

Then one day, out of the blue, someone I had worked with briefly in the federal government recommended me for a job at a consumer products company that was looking for a lawyer with my substantive expertise. I didn't know a single lawyer who had ever practiced law in-house at a company. I had no idea what the job would entail. But when I was offered the job, I accepted it.

A number of years later, while I was on maternity leave with my first son, a friend recommended me for a job as General Counsel of a major company. A job like that would be a major career coup. But I had a newborn and had yet to get a full night's sleep. I had no idea how I could manage that job and motherhood. I would be building my reputation at the company from scratch, in a role that would be new and challenging for me. Despite those concerns, I took the job.

After my second son was born (with some health issues), it was hard to juggle the "big job" and my family responsibilities. My husband and I decided to leave our well-paying jobs in the big city, with its high cost of living, long commutes, and expensive private schools, and raise our sons in a small town with a simpler lifestyle. There were no "real" jobs there, so we both decided to start our own businesses (crazy, I know!).

I started a mediation practice, which I thought was a natural fit for my experience and skills. But despite two years of consistent marketing, the business was only a very marginal success (if you can call $30,000 a year a success). I shut down the business, not really knowing what I was going to do next.

About that time, a work colleague, who was also a good friend, approached me with a business idea: creating conferences for law firms about marketing to in-house counsel. Again, I thought this business was a natural. The two of us were thought leaders in the field. We both had extensive networks from which to draw speakers and attendees.

Despite that, the business was an abject failure. It turned out that the conference business is more about event planning than it is about content creation. Event planning was not the Right Work for either of us!

With savings running low, I came up with the idea for a business that would train women lawyers how to market their practices. My idea was to bring together groups of women partners from large law firms to teach them how to get more clients. After all, when I was an in-house lawyer, I had hired many outside lawyers, and I knew what affected that decision.

Many people counseled me that it was a crazy idea. No one had ever focused on this niche market before, they pointed out. Business development was not a trainable skill, they argued. Most damningly, they said direct competitors would never sit in a room and share their business development strategies.

I didn't have a good answer to any of those concerns. I just had a gut feeling that there were plenty of women partners who needed this type of training and would be willing to pay for it. Unlike their male counterparts, I thought they would be supportive of each other's efforts. It turned out I was right. For the next twenty years, that business was more successful than I had ever imagined.

As I learned first-hand, taking risks, even though they don't always work out, is often critical to propel your career forward.

Taking risks can have a major positive impact on your career. Kate White, the former Editor-in-Chief of *Cosmopolitan*, author of *The Gutsy Girl Handbook: Your Manifesto for Success*, and a *New York Times* bestselling suspense novelist told me, "Every good thing that's happened to me has come from taking a risk. Risk-taking is critical because taking risks means that you're executing big ideas, and that's how big things happen."

Taking risks, even when they're not successful, can improve your self-confidence. As Mary Cranston, a board member on eight public company boards, the former CEO of a global law firm, and one of my mentors, says, "There's a lot of research that shows that taking risks actually correlates with happiness. If you take a risk, it doesn't always turn out exactly as you expected. But that is precisely the kind of vote of confidence in yourself that starts to open up other opportunities."

Eileen McDargh, author of *Burnout to Breakthrough*, says risk-taking increases resiliency, regardless of the outcome. "When you do something you're afraid to do, even if it is just a small thing that you are afraid to do, you begin to develop the resiliency muscle. You become stronger than you think you are."

Yet, many women are reluctant to take career risks—they fear failure, embarrassment, or financial loss. A study of 2,000 women in corporate America by KPMG, the global tax, auditing, and advisory services firm, shows the ambivalence that many women feel towards risk-taking in their careers.[8] The study found that more than half of the women surveyed believe people who take more career risks progress more quickly in their careers. And yet, despite the recognition of the importance of risk-taking, less than half of the women surveyed were willing to take even a small risk, such as volunteering to prepare a presentation. Even fewer (about a third) were willing to take a career-enhancing action, such as asking for a raise or relocating for a promotion.

In an often-quoted statistic, it is reported that women won't apply for a position unless they meet 100 percent of the stated qualifications. In contrast, men will apply for a position if they meet 60 percent of the qualifications.[9]

Part of this risk aversion no doubt comes from our cultural conditioning. Many of us were brought up to be "good girls" who respect authority and conform to other people's expectations. We were taught in school to do the assignment as we're told, follow the rules, and be quiet. As Carol Dweck, a Stanford psychology professor and author of *Mindset: The New Psychology of Success*, has written, "If life were one long grade school, women would be the undisputed rulers of the world." But the good-student habits that made us a success in school don't necessarily serve us well in the workplace, where initiative, visibility, and innovation are rewarded.

Been There, Learned This: Taking a Leap into the Unknown Could Be Your Best Career Decision

Karen Wickre, author of *Taking the Work Out of Networking: Your Guide to Getting and Keeping Great Connections*, was one of the first 500 employees at Google. When I asked her about how she got into the tech world, she told me it all started with taking a big risk:

> I met a very successful computer magazine publisher through a non-profit we were both involved with. When he offered me a job, I literally looked behind me to see who he was talking to. I said, "I don't know anything about computers. I don't know anything about publishing, I don't know anything about the business world."
>
> He said, "I like you. I trust you. It'll work out."
>
> To be honest, I took the job because it was a big increase in salary. I thought, *I'm in a new city. I'm going to try this adventure.*
>
> I'm so glad that I took that risk. It became the basis of my career for the next thirty years. It turned out to be a whole new life that I never would have had if I'd said, "Oh no, no, I'm more comfortable doing what I've always done."

COMPILE YOUR RISK HISTORY

You are probably more of a risk-taker than you realize. Reflecting on the risks you've already taken—like going away to college far from home, learning how to rock climb, or performing at an open-mic comedy event—can convince you to take risks in your work life.

Take stock of the risks you've taken, what Debbie Epstein Henry, entrepreneur, author, and speaker on issues facing women in the workplace, calls your "risk history." Start by thinking about the risks you've taken that turned out well. Remember how you agonized over whether you should take that trip to Spain alone—only to discover that traveling alone is a great way to meet locals and see parts of the culture you would never otherwise have experienced. Think about how difficult it was to decide to move to Chicago, yet that move led to excellent job opportunities you had never dreamed possible. Reflect on how you turned down a job that was not a good fit when you didn't have another one lined up and got your dream job a month later. Recognize that you are not as risk-averse as you may think.

Then, think about the risks you've taken that didn't work out as you hoped. You invested in a stock, and its value went down significantly. You asked your manager to send you to an expensive training program, and he turned you down. You hired someone who you thought had great potential, even though they didn't have the requisite experience, but that turned out to be a disaster. Think about the impact of those failed risks. Generally speaking, even though those risks didn't work out, they probably weren't catastrophic either.

START BY TAKING SMALL RISKS

We often think that early in our career is not the best time to take risks. But, Alexis Krivkovich, a senior partner at McKinsey & Company, disagrees.

> A lot of people—particularly a lot of women—think they need to be overly cautious about taking risks early in their careers. They say, "I don't know anything yet. I'm too new to take risks. I'm going to sit back and see how it all works first.'"
>
> I would give the opposite advice. Early in your career is a time when you can experiment with minimal downside. There's no expectation that you know how everything works. You have a lot of runway in front of you to make wrong turns and plenty of time to come back around and get back on track.

To become more comfortable taking risks, start small. The more you take small risks and see them pay off, the more likely you are to feel comfortable with more significant risks. I always encourage my clients to take risks about 10 percent outside of their comfort zone. Ask someone for an introduction to your ideal client. Express interest in being assigned to a new project. Ask someone you'd like to include in your network to have coffee. These are challenging, but not dread-inducing, actions. By taking these small risks, you can build your "risk muscle" and feel more comfortable taking greater risks.

See if you can "try out" a relatively innocuous version of a risk you are contemplating. Scared of speaking in front of large groups? Start by speaking where the risk seems minimal. Commit to speaking up at your next team meeting or doing a presentation on your career for middle school students. Once you become comfortable in those venues, you can ratchet up your public speaking to asking a question at the company-wide meeting or joining Toastmasters.

Debbie Epstein Henry suggests that you can also increase your risk tolerance by taking risks in areas of your life other than work. In her case, it was hiking the arduous Machu Pichu trail. In my case, it was eating crickets in Vietnam (which are surprisingly tasty!). Taking and surviving risks in other areas of your life can inspire and empower you to take risks in your work life.

The more risks you take, the easier it is to take risks. The earlier you start, the better. After all, you don't want to start developing your "risk muscle" when you are a CEO, and the impact of a failure is so much more visible and significant than early in your career.

ANALYZE THE RISKINESS OF THE RISK

While being comfortable taking risks is important, that doesn't mean every risk is worth taking. You want to take smart risks, not just risks for the sake of taking risks. Before taking a risk, it's important to analyze its riskiness.

Analyze the potential upside and downside of the risk you are considering. Ask yourself:

- What are the potential benefits of taking this risk?

  Making more money? Moving out of a toxic work environment? Developing new skills that would supercharge your career? Having a more balanced life? Being able to do more of your Right Work?

- What are the potential downsides of taking this risk?

  Getting rejected? Being criticized? Being embarrassed? Going into debt that will take decades to repay? Failing?

- What's the balance between the potential upsides and potential downsides?

  Are you risking a lot for little upside? Or is the opposite true?

Many of us overestimate the riskiness involved in taking a career risk.

Lori Mihalich-Levin, a healthcare lawyer and author of *Back to Work After Baby: How to Plan and Navigate a Mindful Return from Maternity Leave,* told me of being offered a job that was a huge promotion. She felt the job was more than she could handle. Afraid to take on the new responsibilities, she told her boss, "I haven't done anything that looks remotely like that role. I am not ready for it."

Her boss encouraged her to take on the challenge and reassured her about the risk of failure. "No one is going to die if you make a mistake in this job." (Ironically, her boss was an anesthesiologist, who actually could have killed someone in her job.) "It's going to be okay. If you make mistakes, we'll figure out how to deal with them."

Kate White echoed this sentiment. "Of course, I was nervous about the risks I was taking," she told me. "But of all the things I worried about, very few of them materialized. Even when they did, they were situations I could handle."

The most significant career risk I ever took was when both my husband and I left our steady paychecks to start our own businesses. I left my General Counsel position at the same time that he left his marketing job at a top-tier apparel company. It was a consequential move, and many people thought we were crazy.

As I thought about taking this risk, a litany of ever-increasing disastrous scenarios went through my mind. We would only be able to afford boxed macaroni and cheese for dinner. We wouldn't be able to afford to send our kids to college. We might even wind up being homeless.

As I agonized about making the move, a wise friend posed a question: "What *realistically* is the worst thing that's going to happen if you make this move?" (Note the emphasis on the word "realistic.") With that question in mind, my fears changed from thoughts of homelessness to more likely possibilities. Realistically, the most likely negative outcome was that we would try it, and it wouldn't work out. Two years later, with a smaller balance in our savings account, we would return to jobs similar to those we had left. It wouldn't be what we had hoped for, but it wouldn't be exactly catastrophic either.

Don't Underestimate the Risk of Inaction

When evaluating risk, we tend to underestimate the risks that come with not taking action. Often when we don't embrace risk, we find ourselves regretting what we did not do. After all, you wouldn't be considering taking the risk if you were completely satisfied with the status quo.

If you're thinking about taking a new job, it's probably because you're dissatisfied with your current position. You may feel you're not growing in your role, you're not getting the recognition you deserve, or you're not getting paid what you're worth. If you don't take the risk to land a new job, you'll likely find yourself tomorrow in the same negative situation you're in right now. You're either going to be dealing with the discomfort of your current situation, or you're going to be dealing with the discomfort of your fear of taking a risk. You have to decide which of those discomforts you would prefer to live with.

I still regret that I did not take off a year between college and law school. At the time, it seemed so risky to abandon the educational track I was on. I worried I wouldn't be able to defer my admission to Harvard Law School and would never again be admitted. (I was too scared to even broach the subject with the Admissions Office.) I was concerned that the year off would just be a waste of time, and I would be behind in my career (whatever "behind" could have possibly meant!). I feared I would spend the rest of my life explaining why I took a year off.

If I had taken a year off, I might never have gone to law school. Maybe I would have pursued my dream of being a producer for public television or a talk show host. Even if those things hadn't worked out, I'm confident I still would have had a successful career. Looking back, I can't believe how ridiculous my reasons were for not taking that risk.

SHARE THE RISK YOU'RE CONSIDERING

You might think that it's a bad idea to share the risk you're contemplating—leaving your job, changing careers, or going back to school. But Debbie Epstein Henry disagrees.

I've had hundreds of conversations with people considering career risks. I'm struck by the fact that so many people keep their potential move a secret. Sharing the "secret" you are considering is a very effective way to get useful input to inform your decision-making. Trusted advisers—people who know you both personally and professionally—can often help you make a well-grounded decision. They can help you think through the possible pitfalls, understand what other information you need to make an informed decision, and suggest who else you should be consulting.

Not only can the people with whom you share the risk you are contemplating help you in evaluating it, but they can also be your supporters once you've taken the risk.

MITIGATE THE RISK

If after analyzing a risk, it still feels too daunting, there are risk-mitigation strategies you can use to lower the risk to a more comfortable level.

One risk-mitigation strategy is to do what the book *Designing Your Life* by Bill Burnett and Dave Evans calls "prototyping"—trying on what you are considering without fully committing to it. For example, you might start saving 20 percent of your salary, so you can see if you could live comfortably on the smaller salary that a job at a non-profit would pay. You might take a two-week vacation to a city where you are thinking about moving, rent an Airbnb, and pretend that you live there. Before committing to go to medical school, you could volunteer for hospice to see your reaction to dealing with people at the end of life.

Another way to make risk-taking more palatable is to develop a contingency plan so that, even if things don't work out exactly as planned, you can bounce back. Think about what you can put in place to deal with your fears, if they were actually to come to fruition. For example, exit your current job with relationships intact, so if you need a stellar reference for another job, you've got it. Have extra money saved, so if the new job doesn't work out, you have a financial cushion to fall back on while contemplating your next move. Start a consulting side hustle that will at least pay the rent if the start-up you're thinking of joining fails.

Finally, and perhaps most importantly, look inward to assess the personal resources you can rely on to mitigate a risk that may not pan out as you hoped. Go back to the "What's the worst thing that could realistically happen?" question. If it did happen, reflect on the personal strengths that you would bring to the situation. Have you shown resilience in prior setbacks? Do you have a strong group of friends and family who would support you through a difficult time? Have you kept in touch with your network so you could tap into it if needed to find a new job? Do you have a good reputation in your field?

Risks are more manageable when you have prepared for the "what-ifs."

RECOGNIZE THERE WILL ALWAYS BE FEAR

Even after you've gone through a systematic and thoughtful process of evaluating the risk you're contemplating, and you have a contingency plan in place in case the risk doesn't turn out well, you may still have lingering doubts about whether the risk is worth taking. Fear is a natural reaction to taking risks. After all, it wouldn't be a risk if success were guaranteed.

Accept that fear is always going to be along for the ride when you pursue big goals. Just don't interpret that fear as a signal that you shouldn't take action. Learn to hear the inner voice of self-doubt, but don't let it hold you back.

BOUNCE BACK FROM FAILURE

I wish that I could promise you that if you approach a potentially risky move by taking all the steps outlined above, you're guaranteed not to fail. But I can't. Taking risks requires being open to the possibility of failure.

Failing isn't fun. It can be intensely painful and profoundly disappointing. It can have serious financial implications. It's embarrassing. And it can make you more risk-averse in the future.

But don't let a failure get in the way of continuing to take risks. Even when a failure occurs, there are constructive steps to take to recover and grow from the experience.

Don't Catastrophize

Often when we experience failure, we catastrophize the consequences. For example, we say to ourselves:

> I'll need to leave the company since asking for the promotion didn't work out.

> No one will ever hire me again in this industry since I was fired.

> I'll never get an opportunity to work in sales since I was turned down for this job opening.

But rarely do our worst fears come to fruition.

One of my favorite questions to ask the guests on the *Advice to My Younger Me* podcast is, "Tell me about a failure you experienced early in your career and how you recovered from it." The amazing thing is how many guests struggle to come up with an answer. It's not because they didn't have failures; everyone does. But with time, even very significant failures fade from memory and just become part of the tapestry of a career. Most often, the consequences of the failure weren't nearly as catastrophic as initially imagined. Even more importantly, the failure almost always became a vital learning experience contributing to future success.

Instead of beating yourself up about a failure, think about how you are likely to view it ten years from now. In all likelihood, you will feel like my guests do—that it was just something that happened to you a long time ago.

I think of myself as having had a very successful career, but when I started writing this book, I came to realize that I had had many failures along the way. I have written about some of them elsewhere in this book. But there are a few more that stand out.

When I was a senior in high school, I arrogantly applied to only two colleges—Stanford and Radcliffe (the sister school to Harvard, at the time). I was rejected at both—leaving me without a college to attend come fall. (Gap years were unheard of at the time.) Fortunately, I found a workaround that allowed me to enroll as a freshman at the University of California at Santa Barbara. The next year, I applied and was accepted as a transfer student to be in the first class of women at Yale. Being in the first class of women at Yale has enhanced my credibility throughout my professional life. It also taught me the career-critical skill of navigating being the only woman in the room. (There were eight men to every woman in my college class.) It wouldn't have happened without those earlier rejections.

Then, there is the stack of rejection letters I've received over the years. The most notable of those was when a good friend had an opening in his legal department at a mid-sized company that would have been a lateral move for me. It certainly wasn't a promotion, but I just wanted a change. I interviewed for the job but was rejected. I was disappointed and perplexed. He liked me, knew my work well, and knew I was very qualified for the position.

When I asked him why he hadn't hired me, he said, "If I hire you, you'll get bored with the job and move on in a year or two. You're ready for a bigger job." As a result of his comment, I stopped applying for lateral moves. Within a year, I got a job as General Counsel at a major consumer products company, a big step up from the job I'd been rejected from.

I share these stories not to be Pollyannaish about failures. They can be crushing, and they don't always have happy endings. But they almost always are not as catastrophic as they seem at the moment.

View Your Failure as a Learning Opportunity

When you experience a failure, stop and reflect on why it happened. Treat it with curiosity, not shame. Not learning from failure is a waste of a perfectly good failure.

Ask yourself what happened and why did it happen. What can you learn from the failure? How are you going to do it differently next time? For example, did your request for a flexible schedule not address your boss's legitimate concerns? Should you have gotten buy-in from the key decision-makers before presenting an idea at a meeting? Was your suggestion to hire a research analyst a good one but just not timely, given that this quarter's revenues were down?

Consider the mistake you made as a mistake you're not going to make again because you've learned from it.

Reframe failure as the inevitable by-product of stretching yourself and growing.

Stop Ruminating

Women tend to ruminate on their failures, reliving them over and over again and blaming themselves. An example of this was my client, Suzanne. When I first met her, she had been laid off a number of years before from a job she described as having been very stressful and not satisfying. Being laid off had been an understandably traumatic experience for her. But fortunately, she had found another job within a few months, and she liked the new role much better.

Nevertheless, in our first coaching conversation, she peppered me with questions about why I thought she had been laid off. I asked her:

Why are you still replaying this? I understand that it was a difficult time in your life, and you feel like the layoff wasn't fair. But the truth is, you've moved on and are in a much better place now. Unless there is an important lesson to be learned from what went wrong (which there didn't seem to be), it's time to let it go and move on.

Continuing to ruminate about that layoff was not serving her well.

Been There, Learned This:
Say Sorry and Move On

Nora McInerny, host of the *Terrible, Thanks for Asking* podcast, shared a powerful cautionary tale about letting a failure overtake your life:

> A woman wrote to me, telling me, "I made this huge mistake when I was writing for *The New York Times*." She had gotten a critical fact wrong in a story she'd written. Because of this mistake, she completely burned down her life. She quit her career as a journalist. She moved across the country to start a whole new life for herself.
>
> I told her we were going to contact the person who had been adversely affected by the story she had written ten years before to find out his perspective on the experience. She said, "Oh God, he will hate me forever."
>
> It turned out he had forgiven her mistake long ago. When I told him what she had done after the incident, he said, "She didn't need to feel that way; she didn't need to be carrying this around forever."
>
> Often, we assume that the mistakes we've made are just unfixable or indelible, and they're not.
>
> I think about this story a lot because I've made a lot of mistakes myself. There are lots of things I've said and done that I wish I hadn't. Every time I punish myself with awful thoughts about myself, I'm just paying for those mistakes over and over again. You've already paid once. Just say you're sorry and move on.

Don't Over-Personalize Failure

When we experience failure, we often personalize it, saying, "I failed." Such an attitude will erode your self-confidence and reduce the likelihood you will take career-enhancing risks in the future. Instead, try to de-personalize the failure, assigning the label of "failure" only to your actions: that email, that approach, that conversation failed. Not, "I'm a failure."

When we do a post-mortem on a failure, we often make the failure all about us. "It was all my fault. I should have known better or done better." But, in all likelihood, your failure is neither entirely your fault nor completely not your fault. There are likely other things that contributed to the failure—your boss was having a bad day or you hadn't been told that the project was a high priority. It's important to take appropriate responsibility for the part you played in your failures but not to blame yourself for things that you couldn't have known or were out of your control.

Move On

Often the hardest part of experiencing failure is moving on.

Early in my career, I had a terrific boss. Once, when I made what I considered to be a career-limiting mistake, I went to him to own up to it. Calmly, he responded, "Can you fix it? If so, do it. If not, apologize and let people know what you'll do in the future to make sure it doesn't happen again. Then, move on. You're better than the mistake you made." It was such an important lesson.

When you experience failure, see it for what it is. It's likely not catastrophic. Instead of spending time agonizing about the failure, spend time doing a deep dive into what you can learn from the experience. Capture that learning, so you can do better in the future. And then, move on. Being paralyzed by your failure serves no one.

KEY TAKEAWAYS

Being willing to take smart risks is an important element of a successful career. When faced with a career-enhancing risk, be realistic about its riskiness. Don't overestimate the potential negatives, underestimate the risk of inaction, or interpret fear as a reason not to take a risk. See if there is a "micro-risk" you can take before jumping in with both feet. With a thorough analysis of the riskiness of a potential move, a carefully thought-out failure mitigation strategy, and the right mindset about failure, risk-taking does not need to be so daunting.

Coaching Assignments:

Put This Chapter into Action

1. **Start a "risk diary."**

   Think about the risks you've taken—big and small. Did you take a class on something you'd never done before—like a painting class or scuba diving lessons? Did you travel somewhere without cell reception? Did you go to a wedding alone? Did you quit a job you hated without a new job lined up? Did you move to a city where you didn't know a soul?

   How did you feel when you took those risks? How did those risks turn out? If a risk didn't work out exactly as planned, how did it work out? If it didn't work out well, what was the impact of that failure? What did you learn from taking that risk?

   Write down what your experiences with risk-taking have been.

   Review your risk diary as you contemplate taking your next risk. That should give you more confidence in your risk-taking ability, and your resilience in the face of possible failure.

2. **Build your muscle for risk-taking.**

   This week, take a risk. It doesn't have to be a big risk. Introduce yourself to someone you don't know at a networking event. Challenge someone's point of view at the team meeting. Take a Bollywood dance class you've never tried before.

   Notice what happens and how you feel when you take a risk.

   Jot down your observations.

3. **Follow the steps for risk-taking set out in this chapter.**

4. **Notice how you recover from failure.**

   The next time you experience failure, whether small or large, write down how you reacted to the failure. Did you initially see it as more consequential than it was? How did you remedy the situation? What did you learn from it? How quickly did you move on?

   Refer to your experience in dealing with failure the next time you contemplate taking a risk. Remind yourself about your resilience in the face of failure.

CHAPTER 4

Say No

A client of mine, MaryBeth, had spent a lot of time developing a detailed plan for how she was going to get new clients in the year ahead. One day, the Managing Partner of her law firm walked into her office and invited her to join a committee that was looking into how to upgrade their library technology.

With much trepidation, she said, "I've spent a lot of time crafting a plan to expand my client base this year, and I really want to devote my time to implementing that plan. Given that, I think I really don't have time to serve on the committee this year."

He smiled at her response and replied, "Good! I actually think spending time on business development is a much better use of your time than participating on that committee."

Surprised at his response, she asked, "Then, why did you ask me to do it?"

He shrugged and responded, "Because I thought you wouldn't turn me down."

Ironically, rather than being dinged as someone dodging work, MaryBeth reported that after saying no to the library project, her boss went from seeing her as a willing worker bee to an up-and-coming star, invested in the growth of her practice and the firm.

It's tempting to always say yes to requests, especially when they come from your boss. But in most cases, what's best for you—and your company—is to set boundaries on how and where you spend your time.

SAY NO SO YOU CAN SAY YES TO WHAT MATTERS

Learning to say no is an important career (and life) skill. Being able to set boundaries as to what you will and will not do is critical to being able to focus on and achieve your goals. Saying no allows you to say yes to what is most important to you.

There are only so many obligations that you can fill your calendar with. Every time you say yes to something, you are in effect saying no to something else. And that something else might be much more important to your career or your life. Saying yes may mean that an important but not urgent work project, a career-building lunchtime conversation, or time with your ailing father won't happen.

When you agree to interview the new candidate for the administrative assistant position, you are "choosing" not to spend that time reading the latest posts from an industry thought leader you follow. When you agree to summarize the notes from the team meeting, you may be "choosing" not to grab coffee with your colleague who is working on a new project you'd like to get involved with. When you agree to serve on a committee dealing with the department's off-site, you are "choosing" not to go to your weekly yoga class.

Setting boundaries on what you will or will not do can be especially difficult for women since, as pointed out in a *Harvard Business Review* article, women are much more likely to be asked to do what they call "non-promotable tasks" —things like taking notes and other "office house-work". To compound the problem, when asked to do these tasks, women are more likely to say yes than are men.[10]

Since childhood, women have received the message that a "good girl" puts the needs of others before her own. Many women suffer from what Sally Helgesen, a women's leadership consultant and co-author of *How Women Rise: Break the 12 Habits Holding You Back from Your Next Raise, Promotion or Job*, calls the "disease to please." But often, when you don't say no, you create a situation where the other person wins and you lose.

Learning to set boundaries as to how you spend your time is critical if you are to honor the goals you have set for yourself. Give yourself permission to say no to time-consuming requests that are not part of your job description or aligned with your goals. Recognize that you are entitled to say no to ill thought-out requests. Realize that you can say no without destroying relationships or becoming un-likeable. Saying no isn't an attempt to slack off; it's a way to focus your time on what matters most.

Been There, Learned This: You Need to Establish Boundaries

Dr. Lois Frankel, executive coach and author of *Nice Girls Don't Get the Corner Office: Unconscious Mistakes That Women Make That Sabotage Their Careers*, says women aren't good at putting boundaries on their time because they think that if somebody needs them, they should be there for them. She shared this story with me to stress the importance of establishing boundaries:

> Early in my career, one of my colleagues would come into my office every afternoon and plop herself down in a chair, wanting to "chat." The longer she stayed, the later I had to stay to get my work done. I needed to set my boundaries by saying:
>
> "You know, I don't want you to think I don't want talk to you, because I do. At the same time, I'd like to suggest that we have coffee or lunch together more often. Because when you come in to talk like this, I wind up having to be here late at night. I hope you understand."
>
> By setting boundaries, I was able to continue socializing with my colleague but in a way that didn't add to my already long day.

REFLECT ON WHY YOU SAY YES

Think about the last time you said yes to something that you really wished you had said no to. It might have been something of little importance—like a colleague's request for a list of restaurant and activity recommendations for a city she was visiting on vacation. Or something more important—like your boss's request to join him in a meeting with a prospect on a day you needed to finish a report for an important client. Or it might have even been something that you wanted to do—like going out to dinner with your girlfriends—but which conflicted with another important priority you had—like getting a good night's sleep to fend off that cold you felt coming on.

Why did you say yes to those things that you really knew you should say no to? There are myriad possible reasons. Often saying yes feels like the easiest thing to do. Or it makes you feel needed, respected, or important. You may feel like you have something valuable to contribute. You're flattered to have been asked. It seems like an interesting (or fun, or career-enhancing) opportunity. For many of us, it's just our automatic, default response.

On the flip side, saying no can be hard. It can be awkward. You may feel like you don't really have a choice—after all, it's your boss asking. Or maybe you don't want to damage an important relationship—with a boss, a co-worker, a partner, or a friend. You may feel like you don't really have a good reason not to do it, or you're concerned that you will never get asked again for a similar opportunity. The list goes on and on.

To be sure, there can be real consequences from saying no. Your boss may be irritated. Your co-worker may feel that you are not pulling your weight. Your partner may be angry. Your friend may be disappointed.

But you can say no. As Carol Frohlinger, a negotiation expert and co-author of *Nice Girls Just Don't Get It: 99 Ways to Win the Respect You Deserve, The Success You Earned, and the Life You Want*, says, "Just because somebody asked doesn't mean that you have to do it."

FIGURE OUT WHETHER TO SAY YES OR NO

Part of the challenge of setting boundaries is knowing when you should say yes and when you can (or should) say no. It helps to have strategies to guide your decision.

Don't Say Yes Automatically

It's perfectly legitimate to give yourself time to reflect on whether you want to agree to a request. All you need to say is, "Let me think about it," or "Can I get back to you by noon?"

This may take some practice. Often, yes has been our default response for so long that whenever someone asks us to do something, we agree without even thinking about it.

Know What Your Yes Is

Before you can figure out how to respond to a request, you need to have a clear sense of what your yes is. Your yes is your priorities—those things that are so important to you or your career that you don't want to compromise on them. It might be working on projects that will get you promoted or making it to your softball practice on Wednesday night. Once you are clear on your priorities, you can decide if saying yes to a request is going to interfere with them.

Evaluate the Impact the Yes or No Will Have On You

Consider these factors:

- What will you get by saying yes?

   Will it move you towards an important goal of yours? For example, building a relationship with someone who may be helpful in your career? Will it show your team that you're invested in its success? Is it something you've always wanted to try?

- How might saying yes interfere with your priorities?

   Will an important, but non-urgent, work project not get done? Will the time you want to invest in nurturing a relationship be short-circuited? Will your

Spanish lessons or your volunteer activities with Habitat for Humanity be given short shrift?

- How long will it take to do what has been requested?

  Try to quantify the commitment you are agreeing to. If it's something that can be done quickly, maybe it's not worth saying no. But more often than not, we severely underestimate the actual time it will take to do something (realistically, triple the time you think it will).

- How did it turn out the last time you said yes to a similar request?

  The last time you agreed to sit at the company's table at a charity event, was it an opportunity to chat with the CEO, or were there only accountants from the purchasing department there? Did you learn about important new initiatives the company was considering, or was the conversation dull and uncomfortable? Was the requester grateful for your help, or was he just happy to cross that item off his to-do list?

- Would you say yes if it had to be done tomorrow?

  If your answer to do it tomorrow would be no, the answer should be no to a commitment in the far-off future. Because eventually, it will be tomorrow!

This last question is very important. Too often we say yes to things because we think we'll have more time in the future than we do now. But the truth is, the future usually doesn't look very different than the present. The time-pressure you are feeling today will likely be the same in the future. Whatever the constraints are to doing it tomorrow are probably the same constraints that you'll feel six months from now.

A number of years ago, I was invited to give a speech in Paris. When deciding whether or not to accept the invitation, I failed to ask myself the "Would you say yes if it were tomorrow?" question. Despite the fact that at the time I was crazy-busy juggling my work and family responsibilities, I enthusiastically accepted the invitation. Who would turn down an all-expense paid trip to Paris!

The picture in my mind when I said yes was I'd spend a week in Paris, and it'd be wonderful. The speech would take a few hours to prepare and give, and the rest of the time I'd hang out in museums, eat croissants, and do some shopping. Every night I would have a leisurely meal, and I'd end the night with a relaxing bubble bath. But when the day arrived to go to Paris, my schedule was as packed as it had been six months before when I had accepted the invitation. There was to be no week in Paris. There was only an eleven-hour, cramped flight to Paris, an overnight stay in a generic airport hotel, a presentation that had taken several days to prepare, and a return flight home right after the speech. Had I focused on the "Would I do it tomorrow?" question, I never would have agreed to it in the first place.

Assuming you decide you want to say no, you then need to figure out the realistic impact that no will have on the other person. Will they be devastated, label you a prima donna, or never present you with a similar opportunity in the future? Will you damage an important relationship, get dinged in your review for not being a team player, or get fired? Will your failure to participate sink the project?

Or will they understand if you explain why you need to say no? Will they be disappointed but not crushed? Will they just shoot off another email to ask someone else to do it, do it themselves, or decide it wasn't worth doing in the first place? Or will they just not care? As well-known productivity expert, Laura Vanderkam, says in her book, *Off the Clock: Feel Less Busy While Getting More Done*, "The most common reaction other people have to your shedding an obligation is nothing."

When someone asks us to do something, we assume the task must be important, but that's often not the case. As a Chief Legal Officer, I was routinely invited to participate in meetings, but when I asked what they hoped I could contribute at the meeting, they often realized I wasn't needed after all. We also overestimate the amount of thought the person asking put into choosing you as the person to ask. Maybe you were just the first person your manager ran into when an idea popped into her head. Or maybe she hadn't taken the time to consider who might best handle this task. If you say no, she might just ask someone else—someone who is possibly better suited to the task.

There are certainly many situations in which you can't realistically say no. But there are many situations (probably many more than you realize) in which you can say no.

SAY NO GRACEFULLY

Once you've decided that you want to say no, there's still the challenge of figuring out how to do it. You want to do it with as little backlash and damage to the relationship as possible.

Here are four different ways to say no without engendering—or at least lessening—a negative response.

The "Positive No"

Caroline Webb, a former partner at McKinsey & Company, draws on psychology, behavioral economics, and neuroscience in her book *How to Have a Good Day: Harness the Power of Behavioral Science to Transform Your Working Life,* in recommending the Positive No as a way to elicit the best possible response when you turn down a request. Her Positive No formula has the following steps:

1. Start with Warmth—acknowledge and appreciate the request
2. Share Your Yes—highlight the priority which necessitates your turning down the request

3. Say Your No—express your regret at not being able to say yes to the request
4. End with Warmth—express warm wishes for their success

Let's say you're asked to come to a meeting that interferes with your getting an important report for a client finished. A Positive No could sound like this:

> Thank you so much for asking me to join the meeting. I'm honored you thought that I'd be a useful contributor. (Warmth) At the moment, I am working on an important report for a major client and the deadline is Friday. (Your Yes) As a result, I'm sorry that I can't come to the meeting. (Your No) I hope you get some great ideas about how to market your new product. (Warmth)

The "Alternative No"

Another way to say no is to agree to help but in a way that is different than the one requested. This version of no is based on Judith McClure's approach in her book *Civilized Assertiveness for Women*. With this approach, you're not giving the person precisely what they asked for, but you're demonstrating your willingness to help. Using the Alternative No to turn down a request to attend a meeting might sound like this:

- The "Partial No"—"I would be happy to participate on Zoom, but I can't be out of the office today."
- The "Not Now No"—"I can participate if we move it to Friday, when my schedule is more open."
- The "Someone Else No"—"I'd be happy to ask Jack if he is available to attend. That way our team would be represented at the meeting."
- The "Time-Blocked No"—"I can participate for the first half hour, but I'm busy preparing the year-end financials, so I can't stay the whole time."
- The "No Unless"—"I can do it if I'm not responsible for doing the post-meeting follow-up. I just have too much on my plate right now to be able to do it."

The "Personal Policy No"

Saying no can be easier when you cite a Personal Policy for why you are saying no to a request. For example, "I don't respond to emails on Sunday. Sundays are devoted to family activities." Or "I don't attend meetings that don't have an agenda. I've found that they just aren't productive."

Think about the Personal Policies you might adopt. What conditions need to be met for you to say yes?

Here are some examples of Personal Policies I adopted over the years:

- I only interview candidates for a new position if there are at least two women in the pool.

- I don't take red-eye flights because they wreak havoc on the rest of my week.
- I don't schedule meetings or calls on Wednesday afternoon because that is my time to focus on "big picture" initiatives.
- I only agree to take meeting notes if the task is shared equally among all my colleagues.
- I don't schedule calls before 9:00 a.m. because I exercise in the morning.
- I get home in time to have dinner with my family, even though that means I have to work afterwards.
- I don't have dinner with colleagues when I travel because I need downtime after a full day of work. I order room service instead.

The "Just Plain No"

Sometimes the Just Plain No is the simplest and most effective way to turn down a request.

Start with thanking the person for the invitation.

- I'm flattered...
- I appreciate your asking...
- It sounds great/fun/interesting...

And then continue with your simple, unexplained no:

- But I won't be able to make it.

- But I have another commitment.
- But I just don't have time right now.

I have noticed that it can be more difficult for women to say no (at least in their own minds) when their no relates to something in their personal life—such as their need to leave by 5:30 p.m. to pick up a child at daycare or to take the morning off to get a mammogram. The Just Plain No works well for these situations.

When I had a work request that conflicted with something that was important to me in my personal life, I would just say, "I have an appointment." The other person didn't need to know whether the appointment was a meeting with the CEO, going to my son's science fair, or interviewing for a new job.

KEY TAKEAWAYS

Give yourself permission to set appropriate boundaries. Don't let yes be your default response to requests. Clarity around your priorities (and a willingness to say no to those things which are not your priorities) will allow you to focus on those things that are most important to you and your career. While turning down requests can be difficult, with practice, saying no to requests that aren't consistent with your goals will get easier.

Coaching Assignments:

Put This Chapter into Action

1. **Don't make yes your default response.**

   When faced with requests this week, don't say yes automatically. Say, "I need to think about it," or "Can I get back to you tomorrow about that?"

   Use the time to evaluate whether you want to say yes or no, using the criteria laid out in this chapter.

2. **Articulate your yeses.**

   What goals are you trying to achieve at work—like better understanding your customers' needs, building your network outside your company, or learning a new skill? What are your non-negotiables outside of work—like spending time with your partner, meditating daily, or training for a marathon?

   Write down your yeses in your notebook. Consider posting a list of them where you will see them frequently to remind you of your commitments to yourself.

3. **Be aware of the tradeoffs you are making.**

Every time this week that you are presented with a request that's beyond the scope of your usual responsibilities—to take an intern out to lunch, to teach others how to use Slack more effectively, or to represent the department at an inter-departmental meeting—consciously focus on what you will not be able to do as a result of doing that. What tradeoffs are you making by saying yes to that request?

Then, without necessarily acting on it, *realistically* assess what the consequences would be if you said no.

4. **Articulate your boundaries.**

What will you not do—be the token woman on a committee, travel for work over the weekend, or plan office birthday celebrations?

What will you do only if certain conditions are met—participate in the company's mentoring program but only if your mentee is a woman, attend 8:00 a.m. meetings only if they are held on Zoom, or cover for people on vacation only if they agree to reciprocate?

Write down your boundaries in your notebook. Again, it may be helpful to post them prominently so that you are reminded of them frequently.

5. Commit to building your no muscle.

   Say no in three low-risk situations this week, using one of the ways described in this chapter. It can be saying no to seeing a horror movie, when you don't like horror films. Or it can be turning down going out to lunch with your colleagues, when you'd really rather take a walk to clear your head. It could be not agreeing to attend a meeting that conflicted with the company's presentation on the results of its diversity and inclusion initiative—an issue you are particularly interested in.

   Practice these techniques in low-risk situations, which will make you more proficient at crafting your no response and more comfortable in actually saying it.

6. Pay attention to the reactions you get.

   When you turn down a request that someone has made of you, see whether you have overestimated the consequences you anticipated. If you do get a negative response, think about how you might reframe your no to get a better response in the future.

   Write down your experiences and keep them in mind for future no responses.

CHAPTER 5

Invest in Relationships

My relationships have been critical to my success. People I know have alerted me to virtually every job I have ever applied for. The people who told me about openings ranged from a friend I had known for years to an acquaintance of a co-worker. It was a former work colleague who encouraged me to write my first book, which had a significant impact on the success of my business. Most of my clients have come from referrals from former clients. These same clients have alerted me to high-profile speaking opportunities and vouched for the value I bring to the podium. My podcast audience has grown significantly because guests on the show have introduced me to their networks via social media.

Because of relationships I had built years before, I've been invited to join invitation-only organizations like the International Women's Forum, and I've been nominated for (and received) a prestigious award from the American Bar Association, the Margaret Brent Women Lawyers of Achievement Award.

Quite simply, I would not be where I am in my career today without my relationships.

RECOGNIZE THE VALUE OF RELATIONSHIPS TO YOUR CAREER

Having genuine, mutually beneficial relationships is the key to career success. As Lisa Horowitz, founder of the Attorney Talent Strategy Group, puts it, "Relationships are the grease and the glue that help you build your career." And yet, people tend to undervalue the importance of their relationships and overvalue other aspects of their job performance—like their credentials, expertise, or experience.

Here are a variety of ways your relationships can bolster your career.

Provide Information That's Not Googleable

These days you can google almost anything. But there is still information that can only come from other people. People you know can alert you to an unadvertised position at a company you would like to work for. They can steer you towards someone who would be a great addition to your team. They can alert you to which conferences are a waste of time and money.

One of the most helpful things your network can share is the "unwritten rules" in your workplace. In rather academic language, Catalyst, the highly regarded organization promoting women's advancement in the workplace, defines unwritten rules as "generally unspoken workplace norms and behaviors that are necessary to succeed within an organization, but that are not communicated consistently or explicitly."[11] Unwritten rules might include whether that "optional" monthly brown-bag lunch is really optional, what's acceptable as a reimbursable business expense, or who you need to have on board if you're going to get your proposal approved.

Brande Stellings, a former senior executive at Catalyst and a diversity and inclusion consultant at Vestry Laight, says, "Knowing and acting on unwritten rules can make or break your career." But since the rules are unwritten, they are difficult to discover. That's where your network comes into play—sharing this insider information.

One of my clients, Jill, a very successful lawyer, told me how someone in her network alerted her to an unwritten rule that was critical to her career success. Jill was a very well-regarded associate who had worked on a part-time schedule ever since her first child was born. She had always gotten stellar performance reviews. She had been told that she was partnership material. But a partner with whom Jill had developed an excellent relationship, and who was "in the know," shared with Jill the "unwritten rule" that part-time lawyers didn't make partner. Based on this information, Jill decided to come back to work full-time. Shortly after, she made partner. Without knowing this unwritten rule, she would have remained an associate and been frustrated about why she hadn't been made a partner.

Bonnie Marcus, an executive coach and author of *The Politics of Promotion: How High-Achieving Women Get Ahead and Stay Ahead*, gave another example of an unwritten rule.

> Let's say that you are starting a new job. The employee handbook says the workday is 9:00 a.m. to 5:00 p.m. You show up at 9:00 a.m., and everybody's already there. They've been there since 8:30 a.m. They stay until 6:00 p.m. The unwritten rule in that department is that the hours are 8:30 a.m. to 6:00 p.m. If you don't follow the unwritten rule, will you lose your job? Mostly likely not. But if you want to position yourself for success, you will follow that unwritten rule.

Give Advice

Beyond providing you with non-googleable information, your network is also a great source of advice. Throughout your career, you're going to have to make consequential decisions and deal with difficult situations. Those things are easier when you have guidance from trusted colleagues. Sounding boards and outside perspectives can be invaluable in helping you navigate the workplace.

Molly Beck, the author of *Reach Out*, gives this example for how you can tap into your network to get advice:

Let's say your goal is to have a more flexible schedule. You'll need to have a conversation with your boss about that. How can you prepare for that conversation?

The easiest way to get advice on this issue is to tap into your network. Use a "friends-of-friends" strategy. Tell people you know, "I want to ask my boss for a more flexible schedule. Do you know anyone I could talk to about how they negotiated a flexible schedule? Would you be willing to connect us?"

Provide Valuable Introductions

Your network is your best bet for getting an introduction to someone who can propel your career forward. If you're looking for new clients, they can introduce you to people in a position to hire you. If you want to work in a new field, they can introduce you to people for informational interviews. If you're looking for an administrative assistant, they can connect you to someone who would be perfect for the job.

Advocate for You

Sometimes it's difficult to make your accomplishments visible within your organization. That's another place where your network can help. They can amplify your voice by repeating and giving you credit for the ideas you shared in a meeting. They can enhance your reputation by telling others about how you scored a big sale, creatively handled a potential land mine with another department, or streamlined the reimbursement process. They can suggest that you be included on a high-profile project.

Support You

One of the best parts of having strong relationships is having people to celebrate your wins with and to commiserate with you after your losses. The emotional support of your network is hard to quantify, but it can make a huge difference in how you feel about yourself and your work.

I will never forget the support I got from a female attorney I considered a role model. I was a new mother, returning to work after the birth of my first son. She was ten years older than I was, and the mother of a pre-teen daughter. I ran into her at a bar association's monthly lunch.

She knew I had just come back to work after having had a baby and asked, "How are you doing?"

Despite being exhausted and unsure of this whole motherhood thing, I put on my brightest smile and said, "Oh, I'm doing great!"

She countered, "Really? Because when I came back to work, it was really, really hard. There's those sleepless nights and having to be on 100 percent before a big meeting the next day." She went through a litany of the difficult things that new mothers face when they return to work.

I felt so supported. Here was this woman, who I so admired, acknowledging that it was really hard to be a working mother. It wasn't that I was flawed, inept, or lazy. It was just that I was a mother of an infant and juggling a big job.

Been There, Learned This: You Need to Spend Time to Build Relationships

One of the most common themes that came up in my podcast interviews was the need to devote time to build relationships. This story from Brande Stellings illustrates that advice.

There was a team of law firm associates, all of whom were women, who were working all-out on a case. They were working crazy hours, pulling all-nighters.

At one point, the male partner supervising the case invited the team out to dinner. All the women declined. It's understandable why. They were exhausted. They just wanted to get their work done and go home.

> When a woman partner heard about the
> rejected invitation, she counseled the women,
> "You really do need to go. It's so important to
> form bonds, both at work and outside of work.
> That's how you get information. It's where you
> build the relationships that get you the ben-
> efit of the doubt when you make a mistake."

Sometimes, especially early in your career when you're honing your skills, it's easy to think all you need to do to be successful is to be excellent at your job. Instead of having lunch with your co-workers, you sit at your desk, eat a salad, and fine-tune that report, or proofread your PowerPoint slides one more time. But that memo or those PowerPoint slides probably won't have a long-term impact on your career, while the relationships you build going out to lunch just might.

Failing to build a robust network of relationships can derail your career. According to research by Catalyst, one of the primary barriers to the advancement of women is lack of access to informal networks that can provide important information.[12] Another Catalyst study found that working long hours was not particularly effective in advancing your career, but spending time building relationships with those you work with was very effective.[13] Another study found that people who made efforts to improve their network were between 42 percent and 74 percent more likely to be promoted.[14]

Yet, the concept of networking has an unfortunate bad reputation. Too many people equate it with awkward and inauthentic conversations with strangers. But as Lauren Stiller Rikleen, President of the Rikleen Institute for Strategic Leadership, a prolific author about career success, and a consultant on workplace culture, advises, "Networking is not about showing up at an event. Every time you see the word 'network' or 'networking,' substitute the word 'relationship building.'"

STAY CONNECTED

The most common career regret I hear from my clients is that they failed to stay in touch with people from earlier phases in their lives—like the co-editor of their college newspaper who is now the Head of Marketing at a media company they would like to pitch, or the co-worker at their first job who now lives in a city to which they are relocating.

Having to play catch up with those long-forgotten relationships can feel uncomfortable. It can be awkward to try to re-engage with someone you haven't been in contact with for many years. The antidote to this? Make staying connected a priority. As Karen Wickre, author of *Taking the Work Out of Networking: Your Guide to Making and Keeping Great Connections*, told me, "Networking is more about farming than it is about hunting. Networking is a long-term, cyclical activity that is ongoing."

No matter how busy you are, carve out time to nurture

your relationships. It is an investment in yourself and in your career. Brande Stellings shared this observation about her own network:

> You don't realize how long people are going to be in your life. It's interesting to see that people I went to school with twenty-five years ago still are important to me. My current business partners and I were first-year associates together. I would never have envisioned we would be running a business together all these years later.

The contacts you make now can last a lifetime, if you make the effort to stay connected.

Staying in touch doesn't need to be a daunting task—it can be as simple as sending one person each week a quick "catching up" email. Ideas for staying in touch with your network on a regular basis are limited only by your imagination.

Many years ago, I developed a habit of writing a "Year in Review" email that I send to about seventy-five connections every January. It includes ten highlights of my year, two or three sentences about each. Simple to write, simple to read. I hear back from many of the recipients—and often with updates on their lives. It may be the only contact I have with them all year, but because of that connection, I would feel comfortable reaching out to them for an introduction or advice.

Here are nine other possible ways to stay in touch:

- Forward an article of interest.
- Comment on a LinkedIn update or a social media post. But make it personal, not just a "Congratulations" or "Like."
- Organize a once-a-year group lunch or dinner with people who have a common connection.
- Show up on a regular basis at the monthly meeting of an organization you belong to.
- Offer to introduce two people you think could benefit from meeting each other.
- Reach out to colleagues in other companies who might be attending the same conference as you to set up a meal or coffee while you are both there.
- Devote one lunch a month to staying in touch with someone who is an important person in your network.
- Walk down the hall to talk to a co-worker rather than sending a text.
- At the start of each week, commit to connect with three specific people during that week—either on the phone, by email, or with a text. By doing this, they'll be top of mind for a topic to connect on.

Despite what I've said about how awkward it can feel to get back in touch with someone you haven't been in contact with for a long time, do it anyway. In my experience, assuming that the outreach is not too transactional ("Hey, I'm calling out of the blue to see if you could do me a big favor"), people are actually happy to hear from you.

If the friendship was genuine in the first place, you may be surprised at how easy it is to pick up where you left off.

I recently noticed that someone I had known and liked in college (some forty years ago!) had looked at my profile on LinkedIn. It turned out that he lives in the same city I do. Even though I hadn't been in touch with him for a very long time, I sent him a message and asked if he would like to get together for coffee. He was delighted to hear from me and suggested lunch. It was a long, memory-filled conversation. We agreed to keep in touch.

Kelly Hoey, a recognized expert on networking and author of *Build Your Dream Network: Forging Powerful Relationships in a Hyper-Connected World*, recounted how pleasurable re-connecting with someone she had lost track of can be:

> I recently got a message out of the blue from a woman who had worked with me seven years ago. She was an intern when I had a start-up accelerator that was focused on investing in female founders.
>
> She wrote that she had just returned from a pitch event for female founders. She said it brought back a flood of fond memories of the summer when she had worked with me. She shared how much that internship had meant to her. It was the loveliest note. And that's all it took to re-connect from seven years ago.

RECIPROCATE

As important as it is to build and nurture a network that you can access when you need help, it's also important to recognize that networks are reciprocal. You should be available to provide those in your network with information, advice, introductions, support, and advocacy. The more you do this, the stronger the relationship gets.

I always try to make myself available to clients who call for advice or encouragement. Some call about a marketing challenge they are facing, a sticky client situation they are dealing with, or about whether they should pursue an opportunity they've been offered. Some of these conversations can take well over an hour, time I would usually charge for my consulting services. But I am happy to provide my advice gratis because I like them, and I know that it will strengthen our relationship.

Be on the lookout for ways that you can help people in your network. It's an investment worth making.

EXPAND YOUR NETWORK TO SERVE YOUR GOALS

If you're like most people, your network is probably relatively happenstance—made up of people you've worked with, classmates from school, friends, and other people you know from the various aspects of your life. These happenstance networks are likely to be less helpful to your career than you might think.

In all likelihood, because of the happenstance nature of your relationships, the people you are connected to are a lot like you. If you're an architect, you tend to know a lot of other architects—classmates, co-workers, and members of professional organizations you belong to. If you live in Dallas, most of the people you know also live in Dallas. If you work for Wells Fargo, you're likely to know lots of others who work there. If you just let your relationships develop organically, you'll probably find yourself being surrounded by people who are similar to you in terms of age, stage of life, education, industry, and race.

It's also likely that many of the people in your happenstance network know each other. My friend Susan knows my friend Joan because I invited them both to go on a "girlfriends' weekend" a number of years ago. My colleague Claire knows my colleague Bob because we all worked together twenty years ago.

Also, if you are like most women, your network is likely to be what a *Harvard Business Review* article called a "girls club."[15] In other words, it's made up largely of other women. While having a network of mostly women is certainly comfortable, including more men in your network has clear benefits. As Alexis Krivkovich, a McKinsey partner, told me:

> It isn't as easy and it's not going to feel as natural, but it's really important to include men in your network. The challenge with women's networks (which are mostly made of women) is that most senior leaders are men. Since having the support and sponsorship

of senior leaders is key to career success, if you are going to advance in your career, you need to have a significant number of men in your network who can advocate on your behalf.

The problem with "happenstance networks" is that they are not broad enough to provide you with the exposure to the new opportunities and perspectives that you need to grow your career. The remedy to this is to intentionally and strategically expand your network with an eye on your career goals.

Map Your Current Network

Most people underestimate how many people they already know who could help them reach their career goals. To avoid this miscalculation and to see where the "holes" are in your existing network, it's helpful to actually "map" who is in your current network—to simply make a list of who you know who could be helpful in your career.

One way to map your network is to take a look at your various sources of information about who you know—the people in your phone Contacts, your connections on LinkedIn, and your friends on social media.

Another way to map your network is to think about:

- Who do you work with or have worked with?
- Who do you know from organizations you are actively involved with?

- Who do you discuss work-related issues with?
- Who has introduced you to a new contact?
- Who has given you great advice or a meaningful compliment?
- Who has pushed you to do something outside your comfort zone (these people can be especially important to identify since they are encouraging you to grow)?

Recognize the Value of Casual Relationships

A hallmark of many women's networks of relationships is that they are "heavy, deep, and real"—meaning they are made up of close-knit relationships where the women support and confide in each other. While such relationships are very comfortable, they may not be all you need to succeed in your career.

Having a broad network of relatively casual relationships has significant advantages when it comes to helping you achieve your career goals. Let's say you're looking for a new job. A study found that at least 70 percent of all professional jobs are found through people you know.[16] But only 17 percent of those people are people you know well.[17] It may seem counterintuitive that a casual acquaintance may be more helpful to you in finding a job than your best friend, but because the people you know well tend to know the same people you know (like the Joan and Susan example mentioned earlier), they have less access to the broader web of relationships that you need to find new opportunities.

As Kelly Hoey explained to me, "Deep networks are needed for feedback, advice, and support. Broader networks are needed to connect you to opportunities and ideas that come from beyond the connections of your close, inner circle. Recognize that you need both."

Research published in the *Harvard Business Review* reinforces Hoey's point. The study looked at the networks of the most successful women in a prestigious MBA program.[18] ("Success" was defined as landing an executive leadership position after graduation.) The most successful women had a broad network of people who themselves had broad networks. In addition, they had an inner circle of close female friends who had their back and who they could be more vulnerable with.

Broaden Your Network

With a map of your current network in hand and a recognition of the importance of a broad network of relationships, it's time to think about who else it would be helpful to know to support your career goals. You aren't looking to form new relationships merely for the purpose of having more connections in your LinkedIn network. The purpose of developing these new relationships is to further your career goals. You want to be intentional and strategic about who you are going to add to your network.

For example, if your goal is to get promoted at your current company, think about who besides your boss would be helpful to know. It might be someone who has recently been promoted to that position on another team. They can clue you in on who you need to impress. It might be an ally in HR who can alert you to new job openings before they are posted. It might be someone who excels at reading a financial statement, a skill you need to develop to get promoted.

Let's say that your goal is to become partner at a management consulting firm. Who can give you advice on what the criteria are for being considered "partner material"? Who can help you get the assignments you need to prove you have the skills needed to become a partner? Who can advocate for you before the partner selection committee?

Once you're clear on the types of people or a specific person that you want to build a relationship with, you need to figure out how to do that.

The first place to start is with your existing network. Ask people you know to introduce you to people you want to know. Let's say that you want to add people in your industry but not at your company to your network. You might ask a colleague to let you tag along to the next industry conference and have her introduce you to people she knows. If you are looking to explore a new field, ask your friends if they know anyone who works in that field who they could introduce you to.

Another way to expand your network is to participate in activities that bring you in contact with people you might like to have in your network. For example, if you are a software engineer in a small company, you might join a group like Women in Tech to meet software engineers at larger companies. A similar strategy can work within your company. If you want to meet more people within your company, take advantage of training programs that the company offers, participate in a company-sponsored community service project, or join an affinity group at the company. You're likely to get exposure to people who you would otherwise not have met.

Building a targeted, broad, and heterogenous network of relationships takes intentional action and can feel uncomfortable. But it is important because of the different opportunities and the diversity of perspectives it provides. A diverse network with men, people who are older and younger than you, people outside your company and outside your industry, and people who come from different backgrounds can open up connections and possibilities that a narrower network never will. Put another way, in building your network, variety trumps quantity.

Follow-up With People You Meet

The biggest mistake that people make in their networking efforts is the failure to follow-up once they've met someone. As Kelly Hoey emphasized, "It's in the follow-up that you start to get 'stickier relationships,' particularly with people you haven't known for long. Those little touchpoints, after initially meeting someone, that's where it turns into a relationship."

Follow-up can take a variety of forms. It can involve something that you talked about in your face-to-face meeting, like, "You mentioned that you really like hiking. I think you might like this trail that I hiked last weekend." You can alert them to a podcast episode they might be interested in. You can send an article about a topic you discussed. You can invite them to another event you think they'd like.

Regardless of what action you take as follow-up, recognize that it's not the introduction that establishes the relationship; it's how and how frequently you stay in touch that builds the relationship.

KEY TAKEAWAYS

Your network of relationships is an asset of your career that will serve you now and long into the future. The people you know can provide you with information and opportunities critical to reaching your career goals. Nurture your existing relationships. Intentionally broaden your network of relationships to serve your aspirations. It's well worth the time you invest in it.

Coaching Assignments:

Put This Chapter into Action

1. **Map your existing network.**

    Review your Contacts on your phone, social media friends, and LinkedIn connections for the people you know who could help you achieve your short- and long-term career goals. Consider the questions posed on page 107–109. Remember, the people you include don't need to be your best friends.

    Capture what you come up with either in your notebook or electronically in a spreadsheet.

2. **Implement a "stay in touch" plan.**

    Now that you have a map of your current network, come up with some ideas on how to stay in touch with these people on a consistent basis. Add this task to your weekly to-do list and carve out time to do it by including "stay in touch" tasks on your calendar. Commit to reach out on a regular basis to a few people who are especially important to your career at this moment. If you develop this habit of staying in touch with people you know, it will pay handsome dividends throughout your career.

3. **Leverage the relationships you have.**

Think about whether you are leveraging your existing relationships as much as you could. Are there people who could help you achieve a career goal—whether by sharing information, introducing you to someone who could help you, vouching for your good work, providing you with advice, or alerting you to opportunities? If so, ask them for the help you need (more about this in the next chapter).

4. **Identify gaps in your existing network.**

Taking into account your short- and long-term career goals, who else do you need to know to help you achieve your goals or to broaden and diversify your access to new opportunities and more diverse perspectives?

Take out your notebook and develop a "wish list" of people you would like to include in your network. These can be specific people—like your boss's boss or Robert in IT, or it can be categories of people, like:

- People in particular industries—like the fashion or fitness industries

- People in particular roles—like public relations or logistics
- Men
- People who are older and younger than you are
- People of a different race, background, or parental status

5. **Develop a plan to reach out to the people you would like to get to know.**

   Who do you know who could introduce you? Where could you hang out to meet them—both in person and on-line? Then, do it!

6. **Follow-up with people you meet.**

   Always follow-up with people you meet who you would like to have in your network of relationships. Relationships develop in the follow-up. Without follow-up, you're just one more person they met in passing.

CHAPTER 6

Ask For Help

Women are often reluctant to ask others to help them achieve their career goals. They often underutilize the support that's readily available to them. When facing a challenge, such as finding a new job or learning a new skill, their first instinct is to go it alone. If they want to find a new job, they research job boards. If they're becoming a manager for the first time, they read all the books on being a first-time manager. If they're trying to figure out how to draft a great cover letter to go along with their resume, they google "cover letter templates."

But it can be far more effective (to say nothing about more efficient) to think about who you know who can help you deal with the issue you're facing. There's someone out there who can help you deal with virtually any career challenge you are facing. If you are undertaking a new project, who has already succeeded in doing what you hope to accomplish? If you have set a big goal for yourself, who knows the people you need to know to achieve that goal? If you're thinking about moving to another city for better job opportunities, who can provide you with advice about the job market and the living situation there?

GET OVER YOUR RELUCTANCE TO ASK FOR HELP

The biggest deterrent that women face in asking for help is their hesitance to "use" their relationships for fear of damaging them. When Lois Frankel's book, *Nice Girls Don't Get the Corner Office*, came out, she was interested in getting publicity for it. She had previously appeared several times on a CNN show, and through that work, had become friends with the host. But she was reluctant to ask the host for the opportunity to appear on the show again, because she didin't want the host to think she had only built the relationship so she could ask for favors.

Sally Helgesen, co-author of *How Women Rise*, encourages women to get over this reluctance:

> Women are superb at building relationships. But it doesn't seem to benefit them as much as it could. Over and over, I hear women say, "I don't want people to feel that I'm using them." I'm not saying that we should be users in any way. But don't be overly concerned about the negative consequence of asking someone for help.

Some women are reticent to ask for help because they feel that they should be able to handle the situation without help from others. But Shellye Archambeau, a former CEO and author of *Unapologetically Ambitious*, disagrees with this belief:

> No one, I mean, no one, has accomplished anything of significance by themselves. So, don't think that you have to. Go get help.

Another reason women may be concerned about asking for help is that it will be interpreted as a lack of confidence or competence. And yet, asking for help can be seen as being invested in your career. Helgesen says:

> Research shows that the people who are most successful at achieving sustainable, long-term results are people who draw others into their efforts. That means saying things like, "I'm trying to get better at being more concise when I speak. Would you point out when I go on too long?" Or say, "I'm working on being more concise in meetings. You seem to do a great job of being succinct when you're speaking to groups. What tips do you have?"

Often, we think that we're burdening people when we ask them for advice or help. But most people are surprisingly willing to help, if you just ask. People like to share their hard-earned knowledge and perspective. It makes them feel important. It shows that you recognize the contribution they have to make. That is, after all, the premise of this book: that successful women are willing to share what they've learned to help the next generation of women succeed.

It may be that we're reluctant to ask for help because we overestimate the magnitude of our request. While what you're asking for may be a very big deal as far as you are concerned, it may not be all that consequential to the person you're asking. An introduction to someone they know well may open up a huge opportunity for you, but it is a very simple act for them. Giving advice about how to approach your boss for feedback may be a five-minute conversation for them, but it may be a career game-changer for you.

Get over your reluctance to ask for help. Asking for help is not a sign of weakness or desperation. It's a sign that you value your career, and you value the help the other person can provide. If you don't ask for help, you will miss out on many opportunities. If you do ask, the worst that will happen is that you will hear no.

ASK FOR HELP THE RIGHT WAY

Asking for what you need to succeed—whether it's in the form of information, advice, or an opportunity—is a way to supercharge your career trajectory. But to increase your chances of getting what you want, ask in the right way.

Build Goodwill Before You Make Your Ask

There's a reason I put the "Invest in Relationships" chapter before this one. It's important to build up goodwill before asking for help. As Nancy Halpern, an expert in navigating office politics, says:

> You don't want to go up to someone you hardly know and ask them for a favor. People are much more likely to help you if you have a prior relationship where you have been generous with your time or advice or information. When you've done that, you've created capital you can draw on when you need it.

Proactively invest in your relationships so that people will be there for you when you have an ask.

Recognize When the Time Is Right

While you should not be hesitant to ask for the help you need, there are some especially good times to ask for a career-enhancing favor.

- When you've just done someone a favor

  If you've just proofread your co-worker's PowerPoint presentation, that might be a good time to ask for an introduction to his college roommate who took an international assignment like the one you are considering.

- When you've just had a success

    If you've just had a successful new product launch, made a big sale, or controlled expenses in a difficult economic environment, that's a good time to ask your boss for a high-profile assignment or to pay for an executive coach to help you improve your delegation skills.

On the flip side, recognize when it's a poor time to ask. If someone has just started a new job or is dealing with a sick child, that's probably not a good time to ask her to go to lunch for a brainstorming session on what your next career move should be.

Make the Ask Appropriate to Your Relationship

What you can appropriately ask for depends on the relationship you have with the person you are asking. If you have a strong relationship with a person, you can make a big ask—like reviewing your resume or nominating you for an award. If it's a more casual relationship, limit your request to something that doesn't take much time or require them to expend much of their social capital.

In the course of my career, I've received many asks, some I was delighted to respond to and some not so much. It depended on the nature of our relationship. For example, I once received a LinkedIn request from a person I didn't know, asking if we could set up a call to "chat." Since it wasn't clear to me why I would want to spend time "chatting" with her, I wrote back and asked what specifically she would like to talk about. She responded that she was considering launching a business that was similar to mine and wanted to "pick my brain." I was a little taken aback. Why would I speak to a stranger about launching a business that would compete with mine? I wrote back and said I would be happy to answer any specific questions she had, but that I wasn't available to just chat. I never heard back from her.

In contrast, that same week I got an email from a guest who had appeared on my podcast. She said she was considering starting a podcast and wanted some input about the costs of running one. She suggested that we could talk for ten minutes or she could email her questions. I was more than happy to talk to her, and we wound up talking for an hour. Her request was completely appropriate to our relationship. She had done me a favor by appearing on my show, and I was happy to return the favor. Her questions were specific and carefully thought-out. I enjoyed the conversation because it made me feel knowledgeable and helpful.

By making your ask appropriate to your relationship, you'll have a better chance of getting what you need.

Prepare

Before making your ask, Carol Frohlinger, a negotiation expert and co-author of *Nice Girls Just Don't Get It*, advises, "Have a strategy. Decide how you're going to initiate the conversation. Plan how you are going to phrase your ask."

Your preparation might include how you will concisely describe the background of the situation, how you will respond if they say they're too busy, or what alternative ask you could make if your initial request is turned down. The better prepared you are, the more relaxed and confident you will appear, and the more likely the ask will go well.

Make the Ask Specific

When it comes to making the ask itself, be specific. People have their own busy lives to attend to—they have jobs, kids, and grocery lists to think about. Figuring out how to be most helpful to you in your career is probably not high on their list of priorities. That's your job.

Do you want them to introduce you to a particular person they know? Do you want their advice about juggling the demands of IVF with your job? Are you seeking some tips on how to explain a gap in your resume?

As Kelly Hoey, author of *Build Your Dream Network*, told me:

There's a notion that if you ask for general advice—
"What advice would you give to someone in my
situation?"—you're going to get more and better
advice. That's just not true. A carefully thought-out,
specific request for advice is much more likely to get
you actionable advice.

When I get asked for advice, some are great asks; most
leave a lot to be desired. I'm more than willing to respond
to the good asks, but I'm not so responsive to the poor ones.
The asks that fit into the "poor" category almost always lack
specificity.

As an example, a young female lawyer, Alyssa, who is
a friend of a friend, called me and said, "I'm a second-year
associate, and I'd like your advice."

I responded, "Great. What kind of advice would be
helpful?"

"What kind of advice would you give to a young lawyer?"
she asked.

Now, that's a broad request! She was asking me to do
all the work to figure out what kind of advice would be
most useful for her. Should I give her advice about developing her legal skills, working with clients, networking, time
management, or working in a male-dominated profession?
It would have been much better had she made an ask like,
"I'm a second-year associate in the real estate department.
What's the most important thing I can do to develop good
relationships with clients?"

Molly Beck, author of *Reach Out*, suggests that a good ask is something that can't be found on Google and that uses the word "one." For example:

- Do you have one tip for acing an interview with the Chief Talent Officer?
- Do you have one piece of advice about how to get along better with a very competitive co-worker?
- Is there one book you would recommend I read to run better meetings?

It can be difficult to craft exactly what your specific ask should be, but it's time well spent. It will make it more likely the person you ask will respond, and you'll get the kind of help that you need.

EXPRESS APPRECIATION FOR HELP

You prepared for the ask, you were specific in your request, and the person has helped you—that's great! But your job's not done yet. Make sure you circle back to express your appreciation and let them know the impact of their help. For example, based on their advice, did you land the job? Has your relationship with your co-worker improved because of the tips they provided? What was the most valuable thing you learned from the book they recommended?

For a small favor, an emailed thank-you will suffice. For an in-person meeting, pick up the check for coffee or lunch.

If their help has a major impact on your career, like getting you a promotion or a plum assignment, a hand-written note is in order. (People love getting hand-written notes! It may seem wildly old-fashioned, but it makes a big impression.). Or consider sending a small gift; it doesn't need to be extravagant. I acknowledge favors with a book I think they might like—a travel guide to a place they are planning a vacation to, a cookbook for an avid home chef, or a coffee mug with a picture of the kind of dog they have. People love getting gifts, and Amazon makes it so easy to send one!

Expressing appreciation after an ask is not only the polite thing to do; it'll make it much more likely that the person will be willing to help you in the future. It will show that you valued their input and that helping you was a good investment of their time.

KEY TAKEAWAYS

Asking for help is a way to accelerate your career. Give yourself permission to do it. Spend time crafting asks that are appropriate to your relationship and easy for the other person to respond to. Always circle back to express your gratitude for their help and let them know how valuable it was.

Coaching Assignments:

Put this Chapter into Action

1. **Brainstorm a possible ask.**

   Think about a short-term career goal you have. What is one thing you could ask of someone you know that would help you achieve that goal? Provide you with information? Give you advice? Make an introduction? Listen as you practice your pitch?

   Write down in your notebook other possible asks that would propel your career forward. Then, write down the names of people who would be appropriate to make these asks of.

2. **Build your asking muscle.**

   Pick one of the asks you listed in your notebook and make one ask related to it this week. Start with a small ask. Build up your confidence in your asking skills. Then, increase the magnitude of your asks.

3. Be alert to the opportunity to ask.

    Remember, there are particularly opportune times to make an ask. Don't let these opportunities slip away.

4. Follow-up.

    Always circle back and thank those who have helped you and share the results of their help.

CHAPTER 7

Be Visible

M any years ago, I attended an Executive Education Program at Duke's Fuqua School of Business. In the course on Leadership, the professor asked me, "How well do you think your boss knows the value you add on a day-to-day basis?"

I replied, "Well, a bit, I guess. I prepare a monthly report for him about the status of the matters I'm working on. Occasionally, he stops by to chat about what I'm doing."

The professor then asked, "Okay, then, how well do you think your boss's boss knows about the value you add?"

I hesitated a bit while I considered the question, and then responded, "He doesn't have a clue!"

That was a real eye-opener to me. When I thought about how little senior management knew about what I contributed, it made me realize that I needed to be more proactive about highlighting my successes. If my good work was going to be rewarded with salary increases or promotions, I was going to have to be more intentional about letting people know what I had accomplished. Relying on telepathy was not a good career strategy! As one podcast guest commented, "'Work hard and you'll be noticed' is lousy career advice."

You create visibility for your achievements when you contribute in meetings, when you share your accomplishments with your boss in a status memo, when you share your expertise on Slack, or when you talk about your work in informal business settings or at networking events.

Unfair as it may seem, you need to accept that it is your responsibility to make your accomplishments visible, not others' responsibility to notice. As Sally Helgesen, women's leadership coach, told me,

> If you want to achieve your highest potential, making your achievements visible, especially to those at senior levels, is as important as the actual tasks you do. If you don't find a way to speak about the value of what you are doing, why should anyone else value it?

Joanna Bloor, CEO of The Amplify Lab, has as her mantra, "Every decision made about you and your opportunities is made in a room you're not in." In conversations about who will get an exciting new assignment or a promotion, it's likely that you won't be there to advocate for yourself. So, you need to arm those who are "in the room" with the information they need to advocate on your behalf.

The importance of making your accomplishments visible has been supported by numerous studies. A study by

Catalyst found that women who are most proactive in making their achievements visible advance further, are more satisfied with their careers, and make more money than women who were less focused on calling attention to their successes.[19] In another study reported in the *Harvard Business Review*, when 240 senior leaders of a Silicon Valley technology company were asked to name the most critical factor for promotion within their companies, they didn't cite skills, results, or leadership ability. They cited visibility.[20]

SHUN INTENTIONAL INVISIBILITY

Despite the importance of being visible, too often women assume that good work will be sufficient to develop their reputation. They often shy away from sharing their achievements—not taking credit for what they have done, downplaying their own role in a successful project, or not highlighting their expertise. In a study by KPMG, the global accounting firm, only a minority of the women said they had talked about their accomplishments or raised their external visibility over the past three years.[21] A *Harvard Business Review* article gave a name to this phenomenon of not drawing attention to your successes: "intentional invisibility."[22]

I realized I unknowingly practiced intentional invisibility when I was talking to a parent of one of my then twelve-year-old son's friends. The father prefaced a question to me with, "So, when you were at Harvard,…" I recoiled, as if he had just said, "So, when you were in prison at San Quentin,…"

I went so far as to say, in an accusatory tone, "How did you know I went to Harvard?"

He answered, "Your son told me." Imagine that! My twelve-year-old son was more willing to share my accomplishment than I was.

Often, we hesitate to bring attention to our accomplishments out of concern we'll come off as boastful, arrogant, or self-promoting. But Peggy Klaus, author of the appropriately titled book, *Brag: Tooting Your Own Horn without Blowing It*, suggests reframing this hesitancy from bragging to taking well-deserved pride in your work.

EMBRACE THE VALUE YOU ADD

Becoming comfortable with increasing your visibility is first and foremost an "inside job." The first person you must convince of your value is you. To feel comfortable drawing attention to your accomplishments, you have to believe that your accomplishments are worthy of attention. As Dr. Sharon Melnick, a Harvard-trained psychologist, executive coach, and author of *Confidence When It Counts: Rise Above Self-Criticism to Make your Mark*, says, "The first sale is always to yourself. It is amazing how many women downplay in their own minds the role they played in a project or the value of their skills."

Our cultural message about not bragging is so engrained that we don't even brag to ourselves. We don't give ourselves credit for our accomplishments. We barely register the positive things people say about our work.

Perhaps that's because, like our strengths, our value is often invisible to us. We think if we're able to do something well and quickly (because it is a strength of ours), it can't be that valuable.

I recently attended a presentation by a high-end wedding planner with my soon-to-be daughter-in-law. The presenter had been nationally recognized by Martha Stewart and *Brides* magazine. She did a rock star presentation, commanding the room, providing succinct and insightful answers to the questions posed. But when it came time to answer a question about what she charged, she melted. Her voice became halting, her eyes were cast downward. She charged a lot, to be sure. But in the previous hour, she'd established her value. The person she had yet to convince of her value was herself!

The wedding planner's experience is hardly unique. A KPMG survey of 3,000 college-aged and professional women found that only one-third of working women identify with being successful or accomplished.[23] This was true regardless of their age and position.

I identify with undervaluing your achievements. Despite my considerable accomplishments—being in the first class of women at Yale, going to Harvard Law School when only 14 percent of the class were women, becoming a lawyer when few lawyers were women, being in the "first wave" of women Vice-Presidents at major companies, founding a successful business when most businesses fail, and receiving accolades for the impact of my work on other women—I have only recently, and after hours of therapy, "owned" my success. (Even now, I feel incredibly uncomfortable writing this paragraph!)

I just thought if I could do it, it wasn't such a big deal. Besides there were women who had accomplished so much more—made more money, had more prestigious jobs, had greater impact, or gotten more recognition.

Too often women do not fully embrace the value they bring to the workplace. But until you embrace your value, your contributions, and the importance of your opinions, you will have difficulty convincing others of the value you add.

GATHER YOUR VISIBILITY TOOLS

Recognition of your value alone will not make you visible to others. You need to have a strategy to get the word out about what you do and how well you do it.

Develop Your Visibility Game Plan

Start by developing a visibility strategy that will help you achieve your career goals. Your goal is not to increase your visibility just for the sake of having more people know who you are and what you do. Its purpose is to raise your visibility with the people who are most critical to you achieving your short- and long-term goals.

Who needs to know what you do and how well you do it in order to move your career forward? Is it your manager, in hopes of getting a raise or being invited to important meetings? Is it your boss's boss, in order to be selected for an executive education program? Is it the people in marketing, so you will be consulted when the next marketing budget is developed? Is it people in your industry, so that you can be alerted to job opportunities outside your company?

Developing a visibility strategy will allow you to focus your visibility-enhancing activities where they are most likely to have the most impact on your career success.

Stock Your Visibility Toolbox

If you are going to be effective in making your accomplishments visible, you need to be prepared to share them in an appropriate way at the appropriate time. That's where your pre-stocked "visibility toolbox" comes into play. It consists of what Peggy Klaus calls your "brag bag," "fly-bys," and compelling stories highlighting your achievements.

Your brag bag is a collection of your accomplishments and the compliments you have received on the work you have done. It includes examples of the positive impact your work has had on your company: revenue generated, money saved, operations streamlined, or people developed. It also includes the compliments that co-workers, clients, and customers have given you. What's in your brag bag has a variety of uses: it can serve as the basis for the stories you tell to increase your profile or the memo you write in support of your performance review.

Your fly-by is the response you give when asked, "What's up?" or "How are you doing?" It's a short, interesting, five-to-fifteen-second response, designed to lead to further conversation.

Your fly-by doesn't need to be headline-worthy; it can be about a recent project you've worked on or an experience you've had. Here are two examples about day-to-day work:

- I'm busy working on a proposal for Alpha CyberSystems. It would be great if we got the work since it would give us a toehold in the data security industry.
- I'm finishing up an article I've written for *Food Marketing Today*. It's about trends in meal delivery services. I'm so excited because it's the first time I've had an article published in a national publication.

Here's one if you've recently gotten promoted:

- I just got promoted to Project Manager. I'm supervising four people. I've never been a manager before. What's one tip you would give me to be an inspiring leader?

If you don't have a business-related response, consider sharing some personal information like, "I just booked my flight to Spain this summer. I'm excited to see if this past year's efforts to learn Spanish will pay off," or "I had a laid-back weekend. I read Anne Patchett's latest novel. Highly recommended!"

I advise my clients to develop a habit of coming up with their response to, "What's new?" at the start of each week, so they will be prepared with a good answer to that ubiquitous question throughout the week. Brushing your teeth before bed on Sunday night can be the trigger to get you thinking about your response for the week ahead.

Stories are another powerful way to make your successes known. In a study reported by Dan Ariely, the noted behavioral economist, participants were able to sell $129 worth of garage sale items on eBay for over $3,600—including $52 for an oven mitt—by crafting a story of the history of each object.[24] If a good story can do that for an oven mitt, imagine how useful a story about one of your contributions could be in building your credibility with your boss's boss!

The power of stories was made clear to me when I was given the prestigious Margaret Brent Women Lawyers of Achievement Award. Each of the five recipients was given five minutes to talk about a topic of her choosing. After the awards ceremony, I asked several attendees what they thought of the presentations. To a person, even if they could not remember the name of the speaker, they could identify her by the story she told. People recalled that Senator Mazie

Hirono's speech told of the bravery of her mother leaving an abusive marriage in Japan and taking her children to Hawaii as a single parent. Marygold Shire Melli talked about not being allowed to sign up for on-campus job interviews because she was a woman. What listeners found memorable about my speech—which was about discovering your Right Work—was the story I shared in Chapter 2 about how I lectured to my dolls as a little girl. Years later, people tell me they remember the doll story. The stories—which took up only a small fraction of each presentation—were what stood out for the audience. The stories were what connected the listeners to the speaker.

Your stories can showcase your results, your dedication to client service, your creativity in solving tough problems, and more. Here's a template for crafting your story about the value you add:

- Figure out your audience

  Is it your boss or is it a hiring manager? Think about what's important to them. Is your boss interested in the revenue you generated? Is the hiring manager looking for someone able to hit the ground running because of previous experience?

- Figure out what you want them to take away

  Do you want them to know that you develop creative solutions to difficult problems? Do you want to demonstrate that you can simplify complicated data into easily understood information? Do you want to show that you are a quick learner?

- Describe a challenging situation you faced

  How does it relate to your audience's "area of concern"?

- Describe how you addressed it

  What did you do?

- Describe the results

  What happened? What was the benefit of what you did to the organization, a colleague, or a client?

Here's an example of a story you might tell if you were asking for a raise:

Our product was underperforming compared with the competition, but we couldn't figure out why. I analyzed the sales and marketing data and discovered that the markets in which our products were underperforming were markets in which we weren't advertising on social media. Once we added social media to our marketing mix, our sales soared by 22 percent. I think this demonstrates the value I have added to the bottom line and why I deserve a raise.

Once you develop your story, hone it by practicing it. Say it in the shower. Practice it with a friend or co-worker. Become fluent in telling it.

Ask for feedback. Was it concise? Did it hold their attention? What did they take away from it? Was that the point you were trying to make?

The more you practice and refine it, the better your story will be.

SHARE YOUR SUCCESSES

Having a well-stocked visibility toolbox won't do you any good if you don't share its contents. Take the initiative to make sure the appropriate people know about your successes. It's a widely held misconception that your colleagues know what you do and how well you do it. Trust me on this. They don't.

Uncomfortable doing this? Pretend that you're talking about somebody you know who really deserves credit. Or enlist an ally to brag about you. Perhaps your boss, your mentor, or a member of your network would be willing to highlight your successes in a meeting or on your Slack channel. You'll find many people are happy to help you in this way, if you just ask. (This is one of those situations in which something easy for them to do is incredibly valuable to you.)

But remember, if you want these allies to share the value you add, you need to arm them with the information they need to spread the word. Be sure to share the contents of your brag bag and your stories with those in a position to repeat them.

Dr. Lois Frankel, executive coach and author of *Nice Girls Don't Get the Corner Office*, suggests two strategies for comfortably sharing your successes:

- When performance review time comes around, send an email to your boss with a list of five to seven of your key accomplishments. Start by saying, "I don't expect you to remember everything that I've achieved this year. I hope this will serve to jog your memory."
- In team meetings, when you are asked to report on what you accomplished in the last month, share your wins. Make sure you describe them in terms of how you are making the company money, saving money, increasing efficiencies, or helping achieve other goals.

It's certainly not fair, but it's true, that women have a much narrower band of acceptable behavior in sharing their accomplishments than do men. You walk a fine line between being seen as too modest or too self-promoting. In order to get as little blowback as possible, you have to craft your message artfully.

Dr. Melnick suggests that one way to overcome these gender-biased judgments is to focus on your contribution, as opposed to yourself:

Shift your mindset from having the attention on you, to bringing attention to the contribution you made to the organization, to your clients, or the community. It's not about how great you are. It's about what you did for the organization, or for your clients.

ACCEPT COMPLIMENTS GRACIOUSLY

Once you start to make your accomplishments more visible, you'll likely start to receive compliments. Don't undercut the praise you receive with explanations or excuses. As Valerie Young, an internationally recognized expert on the impostor syndrome, and author of the *Secret Thoughts of Successful Women*, points out:

> We do ourselves a disservice if we're modest when we receive a compliment. We're often so quick to explain to people why we don't deserve the compliment, what we could've done better, or attribute our success to "luck." Instead, say something like, "Thank you so much. I really worked hard on that, so I appreciate that you noticed."

Erase, "Oh, it was nothing," from your vocabulary. "Thank you," full stop, is an appropriate response to a compliment.

NURTURE YOUR CONFIDENCE

When you feel confident, you are more likely to act in ways that will increase your visibility. You are more likely to speak up and share your point of view. You are more likely to ask for that stretch assignment. You are more likely to take on leadership roles. On the flip side, when you don't feel confident, you don't offer your opinion, you don't go after challenging opportunities, and you look to others to validate you.

The KPMG Women's Leadership Study identified confidence as the attribute most essential to leadership success.[25] It also found that lack of confidence prevented women from asking for what they need to succeed, including: seeking mentors (79 percent of respondents), requesting a promotion (65 percent), a raise (61percent), or a new role or position (56 percent).

But it's not always easy to feel confident. Fortunately, there are a variety of strategies you can use for building your self-confidence. Dr. Melnick suggests these two approaches:

1. If you are in a situation where you're thinking to yourself, *Who am I to speak up?* or, *Who am I to raise my hand for this opportunity?*, change your question. Ask, *Who's going to benefit from my actions—customers, clients, a team member, a patient, or family member?* Instead of making it about you, focus on them. Take confident action on their behalf. Focusing on other people gives you courage.

2. Come up with a short-hand phrase which embodies the person you want to show up as, something like, "confident contributor," or "inspiring leader." Throughout your day ask, *How would a confident contributor or an inspiring leader show up in this situation? What would it look like? What would they say?* Then act in that way.

Dr. Valerie Young embraces the concept of "fake it till you make it" to increase your confidence:

Don't wait till you feel confident to act confidently. Don't say to yourself, "When I feel more confident, I'll start my business, write my book, or change jobs." That's not how it works. Feelings are the last thing to change. The focus is on thoughts. Change your thoughts, even though you don't believe the new thoughts. The only way to stop feeling like an impostor is to stop thinking like an impostor.

I suggest yet another approach. Consider actions that you have taken in the past that gave you confidence. Then, intentionally take those actions to bolster your self-confidence.

I surveyed fifty successful women about what makes them feel more confident before a major presentation or a challenging negotiation. Here's what they told me:

- Prepare—Whether that means having a clear agenda, a written script (that you don't read), specific talking points, or a well-articulated objective. Prepare the stories or facts you will use to illustrate your key points. Get input from others beforehand about the dynamics of the meeting. Dr. Lois Frankel suggests preparing what she calls a "headliner": the most important thing you want to have gotten across to your audience if you get interrupted after ten to fifteen seconds (which just might happen).

- Rehearse—Practice your presentation out loud. Ask a friend or colleague to listen to your pitch and give you feedback.
- Recall your significant accomplishments before you go into the meeting—Remember the presentations you nailed, the recommendations that senior management adopted, the big sales that you made. (These should be collected in your brag bag.)
- Enlist allies—Talk to others in advance to get their buy-in for your proposals, so you can go into the meeting confidently knowing others will support your ideas.
- Psych yourself up—Listen to your favorite energizing "theme song." Do the Superwoman power pose that Amy Cuddy's research says will increase your confidence.[26] Wear what some call your "fashion armor," clothes that make you feel powerful—whether it is your favorite outfit, bright colors, or high heels. Remind yourself that you deserve to be there. Your accomplishments weren't accidental. You didn't get where you are by luck. You worked hard. You are entitled to your place at the table.

Sometimes the daily habits you have developed give you confidence. I asked the same fifty women what habits they had cultivated that gave them confidence. They included:

- Being organized—Have a clear desk, a clean house, a manageable to-do list. Chaos in any part of your life undermines your self-confidence.
- Finishing things—Work through your to-do list—do it, delegate it, or dump it. Having lots of unfinished tasks saps your confidence.
- Taking care of yourself—Get enough sleep and exercise, eat well, slow down, and meditate. Feeling good radiates confidence.
- Surrounding yourself with supportive people—Spend time with people who are your cheerleaders, work with people who believe in you, and have an engaged team to rely on to increase your confidence in your ability to tackle challenging projects.

Try out these various strategies for building confidence and see what works for you.

COMMUNICATE CONFIDENTLY

When you become more visible, you increase the likelihood that you and your actions will be assessed by others. Whether in a casual, one-on-one conversation with your boss, in a brainstorming meeting with your team, or in those anxiety-producing formal presentations, how you communicate is one of the key ways that people judge your competence and confidence.

Your communication is not just what you say, but how you say it. Research by Albert Mehrabian concludes that words alone count for a mere 7 percent of what it means to communicate influentially. Body language and voice account for the other 93 percent.[27] And yet, if you are like most people, you put the lion's share of your efforts on any presentation into the content—with almost no focus on the impact that your communication style will have.

Cara Hale Alter, a communications trainer, Founder of SpeechSkills, and author of *The Credibility Code: How to Project Confidence and Competence When It Matters Most*, points out:

> When you are interacting with someone, they're taking in a lot of signals that lead to their perception of whether you are credible or confident: your body language, vocal qualities, and mannerisms. There are certain cues that lead toward a perception of credibility and confidence. And there are other cues, unfortunately, that can lower your status.

This is not a book on how to improve your communication style. There are lots of resources out there to help you with that. But I do want to highlight how your communication style can affect other people's perception of your competence and credibility.

For example, you can undercut you authority when you use filler words like "uh," "you know," "actually," and "like." You can diminish your power when you use "sorry" in situations when you are neither sorry nor should you be—as in, "Sorry, I have a question." When you slouch in your chair, making you look smaller, you are signaling a lack of confidence. If you wave your hands around when speaking, you literally look flighty. You downplay your expertise when you use hedges like, "I'm not sure I am right about this, but…" or "I haven't thought this through completely, but…"

Pay attention to the various aspects of how you communicate. Get input from others on what they see and hear. By focusing on how you speak and carry yourself, you can create the impression of confidence and credibility that you want to be known for.

KEY TAKEAWAYS

It's not enough to do great work; great work must be seen to be rewarded. It's critical to have visibility for what you do and how well you do it. That's where recognition, opportunities, and rewards will come from. Highlighting your accomplishments does not come naturally or comfortably for many women. But if you can embrace the mindset that what you do is valuable and that you are entitled to share your accomplishments, you will find your reputation enhanced and your performance rewarded.

Coaching Assignment:

Put This Chapter into Action

1. Develop your visibility strategy.

    Who do you want to know about you and your accomplishments—your boss or potential customers or clients? What do you want them to know about you—that you are an innovative thinker, an experienced environmental engineer, or a thought leader in the hospitality industry? And why do you want them to know that? Do you want a raise? An international assignment? An invitation to speak at an industry conference?

    Write down what you come up with in your notebook.

2. Stock your visibility toolkit.

    Collect some "brags" that you can use to highlight the value you bring to your job. Create some stories you can tell when people are interested in what you do and want to go deeper in understanding your role and your contributions. Tailor your messages for different audiences—peers, your boss, others in your industry, or social acquaintances.

3. **Develop a fly-by each week.**

   Figure out a quick response you can give when asked, "What's new?" Highlight a professional accomplishment or activity. If you don't have a specific professional success or action to talk about, share an interesting tidbit about your personal life. It's an opportunity to build a relationship.

4. **Practice using your visibility tools.**

   Practice your brags, fly-bys, and stories so that you can say them confidently and fluidly. Commit to using a few this week. Take baby steps to get comfortable saying them by using them in low-risk situations, like with family and friends. Get feedback about the messages. Were they succinct and interesting? What did they take away from what you said?

5. **Say thank you to compliments.**

   Full stop. When someone praises you for an attribute you have ("You're very organized," or "You take feedback well") or compliments you on something you did well ("You finished the project in record time," or "Your compilation of the research was helpful"), commit to responding with nothing more than "Thank you." No more explanations about how it was "no big deal," you were "lucky," or "It makes up for how I messed up last time."

6. **Develop your list of confidence-inspiring actions.**

Create a list of what has contributed to your feeling confident in the past. What are the common elements in these situations? Being prepared? Having successfully tackled the problem before? Being an expert? Having visualized success?

Write the list in your notebook. Keep the list handy so that you can draw on it when you need a confidence boost.

7. **Ask someone to share an accomplishment of yours.**

Partner with a co-worker to put in a good word about your "wins" at the weekly team meeting. These don't need to be an earth-shattering accomplishments, just things that have moved a project along.

8. Commit to eliminating one communication derailer.

Pick one of your communication derailers, such as saying "like" or slumping in your chair. Consciously work on eliminating that habit during the next month. Then, pick another derailer to work on the next month.

CHAPTER 8

Get Feedback

My client, Christa, received the kind of feedback no one wants to hear. The Head of HR at her organization came into her office, closed the door, sat down, and took a deep breath. She then told Christa there was a perception among some senior (male) executives (none of whom worked closely with Christa or knew her well) that she wasn't really committed to her job. They based their view on the fact that she talked a lot about her love of cycling.

Lacking commitment to her job couldn't have been further from the truth! At the time, she was working long hours and sacrificing time with her family for her job. It wasn't that Christa needed to be more committed to her job; it was that she needed to change the perception of how dedicated she was among those men who had an outsized influence on her career.

From that day forward, when she encountered any of those senior executives, whether in the elevator, in the hallway, or at the start of meetings, she made a point of talking about the work she was doing and the results she was achieving. As a result of this change in her conversational focus, the executives' perception of her changed so much that within a year she got a significant promotion. That promotion wouldn't have happened if she hadn't been given that critical feedback, if she hadn't accepted it (even though she thought it unfair), and if she hadn't acted to address it.

As Nancy Halpern, an expert on office politics points out:

> Feedback is an important clue as to how others perceive you. Those perceptions, whether they are correct or not, have real-world consequences. When your manager gives you feedback, he is seeing you through his lens. Whether you agree with his perception or not, that's the lens that will determine whether you will get a raise or a promotion.

Sometimes critical feedback can be hard to hear, but if you are going to get better at your job, you need to get it. As Susan Packard, a former senior media executive and author of *Fully Human: 3 Steps to Grow Your Emotional Fitness in Work, Leadership and Life*, says, "You can't go forward in life or work unless you know what's holding you back." You should welcome honest feedback, whether it's wrapped in a bow or not.

Been There, Learned This: Critical Feedback Is Valuable

Lauren McGoodwin, Founder and CEO of Career Countessa, shared a time she received hard-to-hear, but extremely useful, feedback:

> When I was still in college, my sister arranged for me to talk about my career options with a senior executive at the oil and gas company where she worked. I was sitting in his impressive office, and he asked me, "What do you want to do after graduation?"
>
> I had barely started talking when he interrupted me. "I want you to stop for a moment. I'm not listening to your message because I'm distracted by the way you're delivering it. You're moving your hands a lot. You are talking really fast. You're not making eye contact with me. When you deliver an important message, you need to speak slower. You need to enunciate what you're saying. You need to not move your hands all over the place."

While he scared and intimidated me, it was such valuable feedback. Because of his feedback, I worked on becoming a better, more confident communicator—a skill that continues to serve me today.

SEEK OUT SPECIFIC FEEDBACK

If you are going to get better at your job, you need honest, unvarnished, actionable feedback. Unfortunately, women tend to get less of that type of feedback than do men. Based on an extensive analysis of over 1,000 written performance reviews, researchers concluded, "The feedback provided to women tends to be less actionable and less useful for leadership progression than feedback given to men, making it less likely that women will advance to more senior positions."[28]

Generic feedback like, "People like working with you," does not give you a clear sense of what you are doing right—and should keep doing—and where the opportunities for improvement lie. The feedback you are looking for is specific and actionable, like:

- You need to get out of the weeds and look at the big picture when you make recommendations.
- You need to write short executive summaries at the start of each of your memos. No one is going to read a three-page memo.
- You need to give clearer instructions when you delegate a task—the desired output, how long it should take, and who can help if they hit a roadblock. Other people cannot read your mind about what you expect, and they wind up wasting a lot of time without proper guidance.

When you do receive generic feedback, like, "You're doing great," take the initiative and ask questions designed to elicit more useful feedback. For example:

- How did I do in that presentation? My objective was to build consensus for our new project, but I'm not sure I accomplished that. What could I have done better?
- We've talked about several areas in which I could improve my management skills. What is the highest priority for me to focus on?
- You said I lack executive presence. What should I do more of? What should I do less of to exhibit executive presence?

Don't wait for your annual performance review to get feedback; seek it out in real time when memories and examples are fresh. Ask your boss for feedback about your presentation skills right after a presentation. Ask your manager for feedback on how you run meetings right after the meeting.

LEAN INTO YOUR CONCERNS

Chances are you already have a gut instinct about the areas in which you need to improve. Are you secretly concerned that your part-time schedule is not working for the rest of the team? You need input about that, so you can approach your job in a way that better meets their needs. Do you have a sense that you don't show enough leadership in meetings? That's what you need to focus on in your request for feedback.

Lean into your concerns about issues that you suspect are a problem. Specifically ask about the things you are most anxious about. By seeking input on these issues, you'll either get advice on how to improve or find out you were needlessly worried.

A number of years ago, I did a presentation to a group of CEOs. When I got back the evaluations of my session, I was shocked. The evaluations were largely negative, quite different from the kind of reviews I was used to receiving. I asked the organizer of the program where I had failed. He told me not to worry ("This is a very tough group. Everyone gets low ratings from them") and how I could have done better ("You should have done more research about their companies, so that your examples landed better"). Armed with this feedback and acting on it, my next presentation before a similar group was well-received.

Avoiding difficult conversations will not make the issues go away; it will just make it more likely that the issues will derail your career. Seek input on your concerns, even if you are uncomfortable about what you may hear.

GET FEEDBACK FROM MORE THAN YOUR BOSS

It's not just your boss and those who are senior to you who can provide you with valuable feedback. Feedback from your peers and people you manage is important as well. Those people have different experiences with you and see you in a different light than your manager. They can help you see, for example, whether you need to be more involved in managing conflict among the team, be more approachable, or do a better job of highlighting the accomplishments of the team. While their views may not have an impact on your raise or promotion, they can provide you with valuable information that's important to your career going forward.

In my first job managing people, I didn't have a clue what my role actually was (something that, alas, happens all too often with first-time managers). I didn't think of myself as responsible for developing the people who worked for me, allocating resources for the team, or running interference for them with senior management. Instead, I thought of myself as the "Quality Control Manager."

When a member of my staff turned in a poorly written draft memo that was to go to senior management, I literally rewrote every line of it, so it would meet my exacting standards. When I returned the memo to the author, he looked down at all my red marks and said, "If you were so clear about how you wanted it written, you should have written it yourself in the first place." I was stunned at his directness, but he was right. My job was to teach him to write better memos, not write the memos myself. After that, my input on drafts was given with side notations like: "This point should be at the top of the memo." "What is the argument against what you are proposing?" "Can you give some examples?" The feedback from my subordinate made me a much better manager.

RESPOND WELL AND ACT ON FEEDBACK

Being open to constructive criticism is a critical leadership skill. As you move up in your career, the decisions you make are going to be more difficult, and the actions you take are going to be increasingly controversial. You're going to get criticized for them. Now is a good time to fine-tune your ability to receive less-than-positive feedback.

When receiving feedback, listen to understand, not to respond. Even if you disagree with the feedback you're getting, don't blame others, defend your actions, or debate the person's perceptions. Consider it valuable information.

If you want to encourage people to continue giving you feedback, show them that you appreciate it (even if you don't like what you hear). They are both brave and generous in sharing it with you. Regardless of how you feel about the feedback you've been given, respond by saying, "I appreciate you taking the time and the effort to share that with me. Thank you."

Remember that you will be judged not only on how you do a task but also on how you react to receiving constructive criticism about how you did the task. You may not have aced the report or closed the sale, but you can be good at responding to critiques about your performance.

Act on the feedback you receive. First, formulate a plan for addressing what you were told. Then, circle back to the person giving the feedback and let them know what you are going to do about the issues that were raised. For example, after receiving feedback that your reports are too long and not well-organized, send your manager the next report you write. Ask if what you've done is the change he was looking for, and if not, how could it be improved.

Failing to act on feedback you receive is either a waste of an opportunity to improve, or worse yet, a ding on you for being unwilling to improve your performance. In contrast, acting on the feedback shows you are a good listener, you take constructive criticism to heart, and you are committed to doing a better job.

TAKE FEEDBACK SERIOUSLY BUT NOT PERSONALLY

Many women tend to internalize failure and personalize criticism. They see any failure as all their fault and any criticism as a comment on their personal shortcomings. Compliments are Teflon, barely noticed, and criticism is Velcro, impossible to let go of.

Valerie Young, the author of *Secret Thoughts of Successful Women*, described this tendency this way:

> Your manager says five things you're doing well and then tells you one thing you need to work on. Women tend to dwell on that one thing. That's all they walk out of the meeting having heard.

Instead, she suggests, in most situations, see the criticism you are receiving as about something you did, not about who you are. If someone says to you, "That report was inadequate," don't hear "You're inadequate." Instead of being deeply wounded by criticism, see it as helpful information for you to improve your performance.

Sometimes the criticism you receive says more about the person giving the feedback than it does about you. When you get negative feedback, it's worth asking questions like, "What does this tell me about what this manager is looking for? What does it tell me about what customers like and don't like?" When you look at it that way, you see it as information and not as indisputable truth.

KEY TAKEAWAYS

Substantive, critical feedback can play a significant role in advancing your career. Instead of avoiding feedback, intentionally seek it out. Press for the specificity that will allow you to act on the feedback you receive. Be appreciative of the feedback you get, even if you disagree with it, and respond to it in a way that will encourage others to continue providing it. It is a gift that will enable you to continuously improve your performance.

Coaching Assignments:

Put This Chapter into Action

....

1. Identify something specific you want feedback on.

   Identify one behavior or skill on which you would like input—for example, how you run meetings, how you collaborate with other departments, or how you make decisions.

2. Ask for feedback.

   Create a specific ask for feedback on the issue you identified. For example, what's one thing you could do to make staff meetings more productive, fun, or shorter? What's one way that you could ease the tension between you and the people in sales? What's a suggestion on how you could improve your decisions about which vendors to hire? Then, reach out to someone for feedback on that issue this week.

3. **Develop a plan for acting on the feedback.**

   What are you going to do differently as a result of the feedback you receive? Send an agenda with time limits in advance of the meeting? Ask to attend the weekly sales team meeting so you can better understand their priorities? Seek input from all stakeholders when making decisions about who to hire as a vendor? Once you've formulated a plan to respond to the feedback you've been given, share your plan with the person who provided the feedback.

CHAPTER 9

Stay in the Workplace

After the birth of my first son, Ted, I handled being a working mom relatively easily. I had a supportive husband, a great nanny, a reasonable commute, and the financial wherewithal to buy services to make our lives function more smoothly.

But when my second son came along, our well-ordered life collapsed. There were nanny problems, my husband's job required a lot of travel, and my younger son, Billy, had constant ear infections. I managed to catch every cold, flu, and even chicken pox that my kids came down with.

There were many days when I seriously considered quitting. But I never did—and I am so glad I didn't. My career has provided me with so much—intellectual stimulation, interesting experiences, close friendships, a sense of purpose and contribution, an identity other than as a mother, and of course, financial rewards.

Yes, there were instances when I wasn't there for a basketball game or a school play when I might have liked to have been. But very few of those times are memorable enough to stand out in my mind years later. While my sons are all too willing to share my shortcomings as a mother, such as my inability to pronounce Ikea correctly, beginning every question with "so," and spoiling the dog, not once has not being there for an important event ever come up. While I have undoubtedly done things, like all mothers, that will send my kids into therapy, I don't think the fact that I was a working mother will come up much in those sessions.

In fact, I am always a little taken aback, and of course delighted, when I meet one of my sons' friends and they say something along the lines of, "I'm so happy to get to meet you. Your son is so proud of you and all you have accomplished."

To be sure, I am relaying my view of being a working mother from the safe vantage point of having two adult children, who are now self-sufficient. The picture might have looked different to me in the midst of a sleepless night with a sick toddler and a business trip the next morning. And yes, I will admit my exercise regime and friendships suffered a lot at many points in my life because of my family responsibilities and my work and travel schedule. But taking everything into consideration, if I had a do-over, I wouldn't do it differently. Except I would have worried less about the negative impact my being a working mother had on my children!

RECOGNIZE THERE WILL BE CHALLENGES

There is no doubt that juggling work and raising children is a challenge. Sickness, doctor's appointments, unreliable caregiver arrangements, children's activities, late night meetings, and business travel all wreak havoc with your life. Getting your *work* work and *home* work done each day is stressful.

The pressure on women of juggling responsibilities at work and on the home front is well documented. According to Pew Research, more than 60 percent of the households in the US are dual-career couples.[29] But in those households, the responsibility for maintaining the household and taking care of children still falls largely on women. According to research by the management consulting firm BCG, women are two times more likely than men to bear the primary responsibility for household tasks in two-career families.[30] Women are more likely to handle tasks that are time sensitive and occur frequently (for example, picking up children from daycare and making and cleaning up from meals).[31] In other words, the daily grind of household tasks falls largely on working mothers.

Add to that guilt about the emotional impact working may have on children, regrets about the moments missed, caregiver costs, and lack of time for self-care to re-boot, and it is easy to see how stressful combining work and family can be. It's tempting to wonder whether "the juggle" is worth it.

DON'T OVERESTIMATE THE NEGATIVES

The research that Hana Schank and Elizabeth Wallace did for their book, *Ambition Decisions: What Women Know About Work, Family, and the Path to Building a Life*, revealed what some may view as a surprising finding. They found that mothers who were most committed to their careers—what they call the "high achievers"—were less conflicted and harried than those mothers who put less priority on their careers. They posited:

> They probably felt less guilty because they felt, "Well, what I'm doing is important." In many cases, they were supporting their families. They got a lot of financial and professional validation, so they really didn't come across as the stereotypical haggard, career woman that we see in the media.

In my own interviews of fifty career-focused mothers, I asked them what regrets, if any, they had about being a working mother. The most common response was some version of, "I regret spending so much time worrying about being a working mother." (There were also plenty of women who said, "None.")

Not surprisingly, some also said, "I regret not being there more." But when I asked about the specific events they regretted missing, they rarely could come up with a specific example. In other words, they had this vague sense of regret, but it was not powerful enough to have made an indelible impression.

Thinking that you will be there for every important moment in your child's life, whether you are working or not, is an unrealistic expectation. Samantha Ettus, Founder and CEO of Park Place Payments and author of *The Pie Life: A Guilt-Free Recipe for Success and Satisfaction*, shared this story.

> I have a friend who dropped out of the workforce because she'd missed her oldest child's first steps. She declared, "I'm not missing another moment!"
>
> But when her daughter took her first steps, she wasn't there. She was at her older son's soccer game. She wasn't working anymore just so she wouldn't miss a moment like that. But she missed that moment anyway! We're always going to miss moments. But it's a mistake to blame work for it.

DON'T WORRY—THE KIDS WILL BE ALRIGHT

Many women who stay home to take care of their children do so because they worry that being a working mother will have a lasting, negative impact on their kids. But many of my guests disagreed with this view. Gail Golden, management psychologist, executive coach, and author of *Curating Your Life: Ending the Struggle for Work-Life Balance*, went so far as to say:

> The greatest favor I ever did for my three sons was to work full-time while they were children. I'm a very

ambitious, high-energy, and intense person. If my children had been my career, I would be pouring all of that intensity into them and their achievement as an example of how well I was doing my "job." That's not a very healthy parent-child relationship. Because I had other sources of achievement and self-esteem, I could step back and let my scruffy little boys be scruffy little boys, instead of having to be superstars at everything.

Many of my podcast guests expressed similar perspectives—feeling that you need to keep a part of yourself that is separate from child-rearing in order to avoid becoming the dreaded helicopter parent. Being happy in your own life is important if you are to be the best parent that you can be.

In fact, research shows that children of working mothers are just as happy in adulthood as the children of moms who stayed home full-time. Sons of working mothers are more likely to support gender equality as adults, and as fathers, they spend twice as much time on household chores and childcare responsibilities as do sons of stay-at-home moms. Adult daughters of working mothers are more likely to be employed, make more money, and are more likely to hold supervisory responsibility.[32]

Even though it may feel like you are not spending enough time with your kids when you work, Pew Research calculates that today's working mothers spend as much time with their kids as did stay-at-home moms in the '60s.[33]

UNDERSTAND THE COSTS OF LEAVING THE WORKFORCE

Tempting as it may be to walk into your boss's office on an especially stressful day and quit, don't do it! Leaving the workforce for any significant period of time (longer than a reasonable maternity leave) is a decision which has serious, long-term consequences (much more serious that you may imagine the day you quit).

Before you make the decision to quit, carefully consider the costs—financial, career-wise, and personal.

Calculate the Financial Costs

There are both short-term and long-term financial costs to leaving the workforce. Many women focus only on the short-term costs, leading them to falsely conclude that there's little financial reason to stay in the workforce. They think, *I make X amount of money, and I have to pay Y for childcare (with Y being a very big number). If I add up all the expenses associated with working—childcare, taxes, the cost of commuting, work clothes, and eating lunch out—it's basically a wash or, worse yet, a negative.* As more than one working mother has said to me, "My nanny makes more than I do."

Reaching that conclusion suggests that you are weighing the cost of childcare only against your salary. But the cost of childcare shouldn't be viewed as solely the responsibility of your paycheck. After all, you and your partner (if you have one) are both parents of the little person needing care, and the cost of childcare should be shared equally.

More importantly, the "my salary vs. the nanny's salary" calculation fails to understand the true long-term financial costs of leaving the workforce. Kathryn Sollmann, a work-life expert and author of *Ambition Redefined: Why the Corner Office Doesn't Work for Every Woman & What to Do Instead,* cites the Center for American Progress calculation that women give up four times their salaries for every year they're out of the workforce. This is because there is a large "opportunity cost" for taking time out of the workforce for child-rearing—lost income, lost wage growth, lost promotional opportunities, and lost retirement benefits over the course of your career.

When you leave the workforce, you obviously lose the salary you were making. But you also lose the amount of your paycheck you were saving and investing, and the retirement benefits you were accruing from your employer and Social Security. Because of the "time-value" of money, that amount is much more down the road than it is today.

Then, once you reenter the workforce, the raises you receive over the remaining life of your career will be based on the diminished salary you will likely earn when you go back to work (more about that later). Over a lifetime, you will earn considerably less than you would have had you stayed in the workforce continuously. Add to that the fact that women, on average, still earn less, invest less profitably, and live longer than men, and you can see the significant long-term financial consequences of the decision to leave the workforce to raise children.

Let's move this out of the hypothetical and do a real-world analysis. Using the calculator provided by the Center for American Progress, if you decide to leave the workforce for five years when you're thirty years old and earning $85,000 a year, it will cost you $1,155,000 over the course of a career. That includes $425,000 in lost income, $422,777 in lost wage growth, and $307,397 in lost retirement benefits over the course of your career.[34] Compare that to the cost of full-time daycare or a nanny for five years!

That's assuming you only stay out of the workforce for five years. In fact, according to research done by Sollmann, the average length of time that women remain out of the workforce is much longer:

> Women say that they're going to leave for a couple of years. Then, there's always a reason to not go back. Joey's starting kindergarten. Your mother is sick. You wake up one day and an average of twelve years has gone by.

You can quibble with the assumptions on which these calculations are based. But the broader point is undeniable: leaving the workforce for any significant period of time has substantial financial downsides. This should be part of any calculation you do when thinking about leaving your job to be home full-time raising your children.

Samantha Ettus summed up why she advocates for women to stay in the workforce:

Your life is really long, and those baby years are really short. You don't want to be making financial decisions that are short-term gains with long-term repercussions. When you're in those early years, which are so overwhelming and occupying, it's so easy to look at the short-term. "How am I going to get a good night's sleep?" But in fact, these decisions have long-term ramifications, and it's important to keep those factors in front of you.

Finally, remember your family benefits financially from you working. It provides them with insurance against the negative financial occurrences that could have an adverse impact on their lives—like job loss by your partner, divorce, or disability. Based on almost twenty years of helping women to return to the workforce, Sollmann says the vast majority of women who leave the workforce to care for children eventually return. And most return for financial reasons: a divorce, college costs, or inadequate retirement savings.

Consider the Career Costs

In addition to the financial costs, there are significant negative career impacts of being out of the workforce for an extended period of time.

Many women assume they will be able to rejoin the workplace where they left it. But returning to the workforce after a significant break often turns out to be much more difficult than many women anticipate. Elizabeth Wallace commented about the women she studied:

> I think the women who left the workforce thought, *Oh, I'm bright. I'm educated. I have skills. I've had a job before where I did well. I will be able to work again.* I think they were surprised at just how challenging it was to get a job. I think that they anticipated it was going to be a lot easier.

The longer you have been out of the workplace, the more difficult it is to return to a comparable position and equal compensation. In a rapidly evolving business world, you will inevitably be competing against other job seekers who haven't left the workforce and whose skills are more up to date. You don't need to be out of the workforce for long to face difficulties because of out-of-date skills. A study by Deloitte found that employers view the half-life of technical skills as about two years.[35]

It's easy to think you'll be able to pick back up where you left off before leaving the workplace, but the reality is that an extended absence will almost always mean a less senior position and less pay when you do go back to work.

Been There, Learned This: It's Harder to Get Back into the Workforce than You Think

Caren Ulrich-Stacy, who runs a successful "returnship program" for women lawyers at Diversity Lab, shared her experience advocating for candidates who had taken a major pause in their careers:

> Every time I would present a résumé of a women who had been out of the workforce for a significant period of time, I would inevitably hear, "Gosh, Caren, it's too risky. They've been out for ten years, technology has changed, the law has changed, regulations have changed. How do we know that she can just come in and do what she needs to do?"

Factor in the Personal Costs

As compelling as the financial and career costs are for not leaving the workforce, my interviews indicate that leaving the workforce can also take a significant toll on a woman's identity. Even in pricey San Francisco, when I asked working mothers what their primary driver was for staying in the workforce, I heard time and again comments like, "My identity is much more multifaceted than just being a mother." One woman said bluntly, "I'm ambitious; that's just who I am. I need an outlet for that ambition."

Work provides many benefits besides monetary ones—being engaged and stimulated, utilizing innate talents, pursuing meaningful goals, being challenged, having a group of interesting colleagues, and receiving respect, admiration, and recognition. As Ettus shared with me:

> There's a sense of well-being and fulfillment that we feel when we have goals of our own and are focused on achieving those goals. Just because we have a baby doesn't mean that our ambition or our desire to achieve disappears.

When faced with the competing demands of work and family life, women are often reluctant to acknowledge how important their career is to them. They feel it is selfish to put their career ambitions over their children's needs. But it's okay to acknowledge that both your job and your family are important to you and that you want to have both in your life. Being fulfilled in all aspects of your life will benefit not only you but your family as well.

REALIZE YOU HAVE ALTERNATIVES

What's a woman to do when she can't reconcile being a good mother with being committed to a career? It doesn't have to be black or white. There are alternatives. As Sollmann says:

It's not all or nothing. Work does not mean that you have to work sixty hours a week, commute long distances, travel, and rarely see you kids. Today we can work in so many flexible ways—in ways that fit our lives. There's really no reason why a woman can't work remotely or on a reduced schedule that will keep her skills and her resume current.

Perhaps you can "tweak" your current full-time job to make it more compatible with your family responsibilities. If you are struggling managing your job and family, don't be reluctant to ask for what you need to stay in the workplace. If you've built "career equity" (goodwill for the good job you've done), you are a valued employee with a proven track record who your employer wants to keep. Your employer may be willing to let you step back a bit from your work commitments—perhaps by moving from an always-on, client-facing job to a more predictable internal role, taking on less-demanding assignments, traveling less, working fewer hours on a flexible schedule, or working remotely.

Lori Mihalich-Levin, author of *Back to Work After Baby*, highlighted the importance of being proactive in getting a more family-friendly position. She moved from being a full-time association executive to being a 60-percent-time partner at a global law firm. She described her move.

I've had so many people say to me, "Oh, I didn't know it was possible to be a partner at a law firm on a 60-percent schedule." I tell them, "Well, it wasn't like someone put an ad out that said, 'Hiring: part-time partner.'" It was because I asked, "Would you be interested in my being there on a 60-percent schedule?" A large number of firms said yes. There are opportunities to create things that don't exist.

Samantha Ettus encourages "downshifting" as a strategy to navigate those challenging years when children are young:

This week I had two women who work at big corporations ask for career advice. Both were moms of kids under five. One was wondering if she should start her own business. The other was considering a new position that required more travel than her current job but paid better.

My answer was the same for both. When you have children below the age of five, ease up on yourself. These are the "Maintenance Years." Don't pressure yourself to leapfrog five levels in your career. Your goal during this time is to sustain your career and keep your contacts warm. If you can come out of these five years with your network and your resume intact, you're a winner. Don't beat yourself up about what you haven't accomplished during this extra-challenging time in your life.

Approaching your job in a different way may be a way to balance work and family. For example, Mihalich-Levin had always been an anxious public speaker. Before she had children, to reduce her anxiety, she would pour hours and hours into preparing her presentations. But once she had children, she could no longer afford the luxury of spending that much time preparing for a speech. So, she became much less scripted in her speaking engagements. An unintended, but positive, consequence of her new approach was that her presentations connected better with her audiences and were more positively received.

Laura Vanderkam, the noted time management guru, believes that you can make adjustments in how you utilize your time in order to balance your work and home responsibilities. It's just a matter of being clear and intentional about living your priorities. She documented this in her book, *I Know How She Does It: How Successful Women Make the Most of Their Time*. She studied 1,001 days in the lives of working mothers earning at least $100,000 a year. She found that the average full-time female executive works forty-four hours a week and sleeps fifty-four hours a week. That leaves seventy hours a week for everything else—commuting, household maintenance, and personal and family time. She argues that our feeling of being wildly out of balance when working is the result of not setting clear priorities and enforcing boundaries. For example, to make the most of your non-work time, unless these are your priorities, don't agree to make home-baked cookies for the PTA bake sale, and don't spend precious time driving across town to attend your favorite Pilates class or see your long-time dentist. Buy store-bought cookies for the bake sale. Find a Pilates class or dentist closer to home.

In my case, one of my personal priorities was to have dinner together as a family most nights. But that didn't mean I had to spend hours preparing the meal. I became an excellent purchaser of prepared foods (shout out to Trader Joes for making me look good!). My priority of spending time together over dinner was met without the time-consuming task of making a home-cooked meal every night.

It often feels like there's not enough time in the day. And that feeling is based in reality. The simple truth is you can't do everything. Being willing to compromise on things that are not a priority for you is the key to being able to juggle your work life and home life.

KEY TAKEAWAYS

There are powerful personal, as well as societal, pressures that encourage women to leave the workforce to care for young children. Given that, you may be surprised, as I was, with the results of a survey that Sollmann conducted of 600 women who had been stay-at-home moms. She found that most regretted that they gave up work entirely, and the security and independence it provides. She told me, "What they say now is, 'I wish that I had always kept my hand in.'" Having experienced first-hand the financial, career, and personal consequences of having left the workplace, her study found that "fewer than 7 percent of mothers would advise their daughters to leave the workforce and care for young children."

Coaching Assignments:

Put This Chapter into Action

Before leaving the workforce:

1. **Calculate both the short- and long-term financial impact of leaving the workforce.**

   Consider not only the cost of childcare, commuting, and clothes, but the loss of retirement savings and future salary increases. The interactive calculator on the hidden costs of leaving the workforce on the Center for American Progress' website (www.americanprogress.org) is one way to do this.[36]

2. **Calculate the personal cost of leaving the workforce.**

   What will you be losing in terms of the satisfaction, skills, confidence, network, work friendships, and the meaning that your work provides?

3. **Tune out negative noise about working mothers.**

   Challenge the stories that the media and society present about the miserable working mother. Talk to other working moms who have stayed in the workforce while raising young children and get their input on how they have managed "the juggle." Question the default assumptions about what being a good mother looks like.

4. **Leverage your career equity with your current employer.**

See if you can work out an arrangement that would allow you to balance work and family responsibilities better—more flexible hours, less travel, remote work, a different role, or less than a full-time commitment.

5. **Explore work alternatives.**

If you can't work out an arrangement with your current employer, is there an acceptable work alternative out there? If you can't find a role as an employee, consider freelancing or consulting projects that would make working more palatable.

6. **Negotiate with your partner (if you have one) to more equally share caregiving and household responsibilities.**

Sometimes we are our own worst enemies when it comes to sharing the workload on the family front. We naturally fall into gender roles from another era. We assume that we need to take on responsibilities that we don't.

7. **Consider outsourcing tasks, if you can afford it.**

Consider whether meal and grocery delivery, a cleaning person, a pet walker, or a lawn maintenance service would allow you to devote more quality time to your family.

8. **Live your priorities.**

Focus your time at work and at home on what really matters to you. If something isn't a priority, is there a way to simplify the task, get someone else to do it, or just not do it at all? I call this "do it, delegate it, or dump it" thinking. It works equally well at work and at home.

CHAPTER 10

The Challenging Realities of Having a Successful Career

S o far, this book has been about what you can do to have the career of your dreams. I wish I could promise you that, if you just follow the nine steps outlined in this book, that career will be manifested.

But the truth is there are some things that may make achieving your dream career more difficult. In this chapter, I want to address some realities you're likely to face as a woman in the workplace. I share these with you not to depress or discourage you but to give you a head's up about what you may encounter along the way. Knowing these potential obstacles will enable you to develop strategies to deal with them, rather than being blind-sided and side-lined by them.

IT'S HARD WORK

If you've gotten this far in the book and actually tackled some of the Coaching Assignments, you realize that doing what needs to be done to be successful is not easy. Sometimes you need to do things that are difficult, uncomfortable, or scary, or all three. You may be frustrated in trying to figure out how to walk the fine line between being assertive without coming off as aggressive. You may need to do things for which you will be criticized. As you progress in your career, you may feel lonely as you find yourself the only woman in the room.

You may look at some of your colleagues and wonder how it can be so easy for them to be successful. But as Valerie Young, author of the *Secret Thoughts of Successful Women*, points out:

> It takes a lot of work to make it look easy. We often look at other people who seem to do things effortlessly. But I think we underestimate the weeks, months, and years that went into making something great look easy. Then, we fall into that trap of expecting overnight success for ourselves.

The clearer you are about what you are getting in return for all your hard work, the more likely you are to stay motivated to do those hard things. Why do you want to have a successful career? Do you want to be financially secure? Do you want to be respected for your talents? Do you want to make your parents, who have sacrificed to pay for your education, proud? Do you want to have an impact on an issue that is important to you? Do you think the world will be a better place if there were more women in leadership roles?

The next time you think about taking a pass on a career-enhancing opportunity or downgrading your commitment to succeed in your career, remember why being successful is important to you in the first place. It will make all that hard work easier to do.

THERE WILL BE TRADEOFFS

Despite the Instagram version of career success, the reality is that if you want to have a successful career, you can't have it all—or, at least, not all at one time. As one study based on interviews of female CEOs concluded:

> For a woman to realize her ambition requires making a conscious choice about what she will give up, and the criticisms she will face. The CEOs framed work–life decisions like other business decisions: recognize the need to make trade-offs, make a choice, accept the responsibilities that come with it, and move on.[37]

Having your best career may mean that you won't be able to serve a healthy, home-cooked dinner every night or be up to date on all the latest Netflix series. You may have to have some testy conversations with your spouse about allocating household responsibilities. Your passion for baking or painting may not get the attention that you would like to give them. You may have to give away the tickets you scored for that hot Broadway play because you have to be in Atlanta on business the night of the show.

Gail Golden, executive coach and author of *Curating Your Life*, put it bluntly:

> Chances are, you aren't going to win a Nobel Prize if you're busy looking after young children. You're probably not going to be the parent who brings homemade cookies to school if you're a high-powered neurosurgeon. If you are going to be a full-time professional and a parent, you are probably going to do both of them less well than if you were only doing one of them. To be sure, there are going to be trade-offs, but for most of us, it's better to do both.

Only you can decide what trade-offs you are willing to make, recognizing that your career may not advance as fast or far because of your choices. As Morra Aarons-Mele, author of *Hiding in the Bathroom*, told me:

> Meeting your needs may result in less career success than you might have hoped. You may have to have less. Less money, less renown. People often pretend these accommodations, whether it's to work part-time or to take three years out of your career to raise

kids or whatever, are not going to have consequences. But the reality is, it usually does.

You have to accept that to make yourself happy and healthy, you may not be able to participate on the fast track. That's tough, especially for really ambitious young women.

Regardless of the path you choose, it's important to acknowledge the trade-offs that you need to make to achieve your career and personal goals and come to peace with them. Otherwise, you will live in a constant state of frustration.

YOU ARE MORE THAN YOUR WORK

You are more than your work. That may seem like strange advice for a book about succeeding in the workplace. But time and again, my guests cautioned to not let your job be the only thing that defines who you are and to not pursue your career to the exclusion of other parts of your life. Being hyper-focused on work and not spending time on other aspects of your life—your relationships, your health, and your interests—is a prescription for burnout and regret.

Samantha Ettus, author of *The Pie Life*, advocates that the way to make sure that you are taking good care of yourself while building a successful career is to consciously choose to address all the critical parts of your life—career, health, relationships, children, friends, community, and hobbies. The book by Bill Burnett and Dave Evans, *Designing*

Your Life, has simplified the categories to work, love, health, and play. Regardless of which rubric you choose to address your multi-dimensional life, Ettus provides this advice:

> Be attentive to all areas of your life, even though some are going to get 30 percent or 60 percent of your time, and others just get 5 percent. Make goals for each area. We tend to limit our goals to the professional sphere, but it's really important that you have goals for all aspects of your life.

Give yourself permission to get enough sleep, exercise, spend time with family and friends, and take time to recharge. That extra hour at work is unlikely to be consequential, but that extra hour at home with your family or at your yoga class just might be.

WHO YOU PARTNER WITH MATTERS

One of the most surprising pieces of advice that came up again and again in my interviews was the importance to your career of having a supportive spouse or partner (or no partner at all). Brande Stellings, a diversity and inclusion consultant at Vestry Laight, was also surprised when she heard similar advice when she worked as a senior executive at Catalyst.

At one of Catalyst's events, aspiring women CEOs had the opportunity to ask established women

CEOs about the most important career advice they would give.

So many of the CEOs gave the same answer, "Pick a partner who will support you in your career and be an equal partner at home."

The first time I heard that, I thought, *Really, that's your best advice? It's about your marriage or your partner?* I was looking for something really hard hitting and pragmatic, like how you present yourself in the boardroom or ask for a risky assignment.

I now see my naivete. I have seen that who you partner with is so important.

Avivah Wittenberg-Cox, an expert in workplace gender issues, wrote frankly in the *Harvard Business Review*:

The conclusion I've drawn from years of research and experience is professionally ambitious women really only have two options when it comes to their personal partners—a super-supportive partner or no partner at all. Anything in between ends up being a morale- and career-sapping morass.[38]

As was addressed in the previous chapter, in most families, even dual-career families, the primary responsibility for maintaining the household and taking care of children still falls disproportionately on women. A study based on data from the Bureau of Labor Statistics found that women spend 5.7 hours daily doing housework and looking after kids and elders, while men do so for 3.6 hours each day.[39]

A *New York Times* article summed up this disparity in the title of an article on gender roles and household responsibilities: "Young Men Embrace Gender Equality, but They Still Don't Vacuum: New Studies Show Traditional Views Persist About Who Does What at Home, and It's Holding Women Back."[40]

Been There, Learned This: Childcare Responsibilities Are Not Shared Equally

Eve Rodsky, author of *Fair Play: A Game-Changing Solution for When You Have Too Much to Do (and More Life to Live)*, dramatically illustrated this imbalance with her story:

> Right after my second son was born, I was having a girlfriends' Saturday morning "getaway." It was a breast cancer walk, honoring a friend who had breast cancer. We were all covered in pink and holding signs like "Not just a female problem" and "Courage, Strength, and Power."
>
> At noon, after the walk was finished, it was like Cinderella. We all turned into pumpkins. We all started getting inundated with texts and phone calls from our

partners with things like: "Where did you put Hudson's soccer bag?" "What's the address of the birthday party, and why didn't you leave me a gift?" My favorite was the text from one husband, "Do the kids need to eat lunch?" In total, there were thirty phone calls and forty-six texts for ten women over a thirty-minute period—all relating to child and home responsibilities.

These were high-powered, very smart women—one was an Oscar-winning producer, another the Head of Stroke and Trauma for a major hospital. These were women who were willing to use their voices. But every single one of them said, "Thank you, Eve, for making the dim sum reservation, but we left our partners with too much to do."

They left me to go find Hudson's soccer bag, to bring a perfectly wrapped gift to a birthday party, and to feed their kids lunch.

While research shows that millennial men have more egalitarian attitudes about gender roles than did their fathers, those attitudes change significantly once they have children. Of millennial men who were fathers, 53 percent said it was better for mothers and fathers to take on traditional roles.[41]

Don't let your partner be your glass ceiling. Negotiate with your partner to fairly distribute your household and childcare responsibilities.

A white paper on the lack of women's advancement in the workplace, authored by Thomson Reuters, concluded:

> The business environment was designed by men for men more than a century ago. Men are very comfortable with the rules and are often unaware of how their thoughts and actions can cause women to feel excluded and dismissed.[42]

As Andie Kramer, a partner in a global law firm and co-author of *It's Not You, It's the Workplace: Women's Conflict at Work and the Bias that Built It*, says:

> Most workplaces have mainly men in senior leadership roles. Because of "affinity bias"—an unintentional bias to like people like yourself—men feel more comfortable being around other men. That automatically puts women in the "out group."

Being in the out group can feel uncomfortable, off-putting, and sometimes downright confusing.

When I conducted workshops for senior women leaders, I would routinely ask them their most important takeaway from the program. By far, the most common response was, "I always thought that the obstacles I encountered were because of who I am or what I did. Now I realize it's not me; these are the challenges that all women confront in the male-dominated workplace."

To be sure, workplace cultures are slowly evolving to be more diverse and inclusive of women, and hopefully, this trend will accelerate. But until that happens, when you encounter setbacks and obstacles in your career, consider the possibility that it may have nothing to do with you but rather everything to do with a gendered workplace designed by men.

YOU'LL LIKELY ENCOUNTER GENDER BIAS

Gender bias is real. And it is rampant. It comes in many forms—from unconscious bias to pay disparities to sexual harassment. It would be hard to find a better summation of the discrimination that women face than the first sentence from a Women in the Workplace study done by McKinsey & Company and the Lean In organization: "In corporate America, women fall behind early and keep losing ground with every step."[43]

Even when there is no overt sex discrimination, women receive subtle messages that they don't belong. Perhaps it is being asked to get the coffee or take the minutes, being mistaken for a junior member of the team when in fact you are the boss, or the exclusionary sports talk that takes place before the team meeting starts (all of which have happened to me).

Then, there is the pay gap. A recent meme summed it up well: "Men chose higher-paying jobs, such as doctor, lawyer, and CEO. Women chose lower-paying jobs, such as female doctor, female lawyer, and female CEO." That women earn

80 percent of what men earn is an oft-quoted statistic. This number has barely budged in over a decade. Shockingly, according to the Economic Policy Institute, the more senior you are the more likely you are to experience the gender pay gap.[44] This pay gap has dramatic, real-world impact. As reported by Catalyst, college-educated millennial women are projected to lose more than a million dollars over their lifetime because of the gap.[45]

Gender bias is even more dramatic for mothers. The research of Shelley Correll, a professor of sociology and organizational behavior at Stanford, confirms that mothers are viewed as less promotable, less likely to be leadership material, and less committed. They are less likely to be hired and are often assumed to be less interested in challenging assignments or a promotion that would require travel.[46] Mothers also experience a "motherhood penalty" in their pay. Research shows that their earnings decreased 4 percent for each child they had.[47]

All of these realities are troubling and depressing. But it's important to acknowledge that gender bias exists for at least two reasons. First of all, when you hit a brick wall at work—you're not included in an important meeting, you aren't invited to pitch an important client, you don't get a promotion you deserve—it's important to understand that it may have nothing to do with your performance and everything to do with your gender. It literally has nothing to do with you. Secondly, you need to know the subtle and not-so-subtle ways that gender bias shows up, so you can see it when it happens. Gender discrimination can be muted, but that does not mean it is any less pernicious. If you aren't sensitive to it, it can undermine your self-confidence or make you overlook its implications.

BUT IT'S STILL WORTH IT

There is no question in my mind that it's worth it to be committed to and take the steps necessary to achieving your best possible career. I believe that the women who appear in this book are living proof of that. As this book laid out at the outset, so much comes from a successful career: self-confidence, options, financial rewards, intellectual challenge, friendships, respect, and making a positive contribution.

Because of talented, ambitious women like you, I am optimistic that the gendered workplace will improve dramatically in the years ahead. As competent, smart women like you take ownership of their careers, they will thrive in the workforce. Their presence and success will disprove all the false assumptions that are made about women's competence and commitment. As more women rise to more senior positions, they will be able to advocate for and implement more women-friendly policies and practices. They will insist that inequities be addressed. They will serve as role models for more junior women to encourage them to remain in the workplace and live up to their full potential.

I look forward to seeing you take your place at the

table—in the C-suite or wherever your dreams may take you!

With Gratitude

To the hundred-plus guests I have interviewed on my *Advice to My Younger Me* podcast. You were so generous with your time and hard-earned wisdom. Quite literally, this book would not exist without you. Some of you are quoted in the book; many are not. But all of you contributed to the advice shared in this book.

To the members of the Women Rainmakers Roundtable. You shared so openly and vulnerably the challenges you faced as women working in male-dominated workplaces.

To the women of the Yale Mentoring Group. You were a major inspiration for writing this book. Spending time with you every month has given me great confidence in the generation of women leaders to come. Your comments on the drafts of this book were honest, and therefore invaluable.

To my parents, Pearl and Arthur Holtz. You supported me throughout my education and career, never questioning whether a woman could accomplish what I set out to do. When I was four years old and told you I wanted to be a nurse, you gently encouraged me to consider being a doctor instead. I only wish you had lived to see how far your encouragement has taken me.

To my older brothers, David and Jim Holtz. You toughened me up with your endless teasing so that I was able to survive when I found myself the only woman in the room at work. You set a high bar of achievement for me to aspire to.

To my sons, Billy and Ted Marsden, the best sons I could ever have hoped for. You never complained about having a working mother, even when I missed soccer games or improv shows because I was out of town for work. You never protested that bagged salad was the only vegetable served at dinner. You never compared me unfavorably to your friends' stay-at-home moms. I am still taken aback every time I meet one of your friends, and they tell me how proud you are of me and what I have accomplished. And to their father and my former husband, David Marsden, who supported me in my work and who also never complained about the bagged salad.

To all the women, both friends and colleagues, who have supported me throughout my career. You believed that helping the next generation of women succeed at work was a worthy focus for my work.

To the *Advice to My Younger Me* podcast team, Mallorey Doerksen, Noelle Mena, and Liz Smith. Episode after episode, you make the podcast sound great and make me look good.

To the team at Scribe Media, especially Natalie Aboudaoud, who prodded me to produce the best book I could, and Kelsey Adams, who polished the book to make it as reader-friendly as possible. This book would not have seen the light of day without the entire team's well-honed skills and professionalism.

About the Author

Sara Holtz is passionate about helping women succeed in the workplace. She is committed to providing future generations of women with the tools they need to reach their highest career aspirations.

She is a nationally recognized career coach and the creator and host of the award-winning *Advice to My Younger Me* podcast, where she interviews successful women about what they wished they had known earlier in their careers.

She is a former Fortune 500 C-suite executive and business lawyer. She received the American Bar Association's prestigious Margaret Brent Women Lawyers of Achievement Award in recognition of the impact that her work has had on helping other women succeed. She is a graduate of Yale College and Harvard Law School.

Sara lives in San Francisco with her Havanese dog, Kirby. She has two adult sons, who often give her good advice and who sometimes take the advice she gives them. She loves a thought-provoking question, and her favorite thing is a great conversation over a cup of coffee.

Notes

1   Sarah Coury et al., "Women in the Workplace,"
McKinsey & Company, September 30, 2020,
https://www.mckinsey.com/featured-insights/
diversity-and-inclusion/women-in-the-workplace.

2   "KPMG Women's Leadership Study: Moving
Women Forward into Leadership Roles,"
KPMG, 2015, https://home.kpmg/content/dam/
kpmg/ph/pdf/ThoughtLeadershipPublications/
KPMGWomensLeadershipStudy.pdf.

3   Sarah Coury et al., "Women in the Workplace,"
McKinsey & Company, September 30, 2020,
https://www.mckinsey.com/featured-insights/
diversity-and-inclusion/women-in-the-workplace.

4   "Women in the Workplace: 2015," McKinsey &
Company, http://witi.berkeley.edu/wp-content/
uploads/2017/08/Women-in-the-Workplace-2015.
pdf.

5   Julie Coffman and Bill Neuenfeldt, "Everyday
    Moments of Truth: Frontline Managers Are Key
    to Women's Career Aspirations," Bain & Company,
    June 17, 2014, https://www.bain.com/insights/
    everyday-moments-of-truth.

6   Peter Flade, Jim Asplund, and Gwen Elliot,
    "Employees Who Use Their Strengths Outperform
    Those Who Don't," *Gallup*, October 8, 2015, https://
    www.gallup.com/workplace/236561/employees-
    strengths-outperform-don.aspx.

7   Tait D. Shanafelt, MD, John H. Noseworthy,
    MD, "Executive Leadership and Physician
    Well-Being: Nine Organizational Strategies to
    Promote Engagement and Reduce Burnout,"
    Mayo Clinic 91, no. 1 (January 2017): 129–146,
    https://www.mayoclinicproceedings.org/article/
    S0025-6196(16)30625-5/pdf.

8   "Risk, Resilience, Reward: Mastering the Three 'R's':
    The Key to Women's Success in the Workplace,"
    KPMG, 2019, https://advisory.kpmg.us/content/
    dam/info/en/news-perspectives/pdf/2019/KPMG_
    Womens_Leadership_Study.pdf.

9 Tara Sophia Mohr, "Why Women Don't Apply for Jobs Unless They're 100% Qualified," *Harvard Business Review*, August 25, 2014, https://hbr.org/2014/08/why-women-dont-apply-for-jobs-unless-theyre-100-qualified.

10 Linda Babcock, Maria P. Recalde, and Lise Vesterlund, "Why Women Volunteer for Tasks That Don't Lead to Promotions," *Harvard Business Review*, July 16, 2018, https://hbr.org/2018/07/why-women-volunteer-for-tasks-that-dont-lead-to-promotions.

11 Laura Sabattini, "Unwritten Rules: What You Don't Know Can Hurt Your Career," Catalyst, 2008, https://www.catalyst.org/wp-content/uploads/2019/02/Unwritten_Rules_What_You_Dont_Know_Can_Hurt_Your_Career_0.pdf.

12 Ibid.

13 Ibid.

14 Ronald S. Burt and Don Ronchi, "Teaching Executives to See Social Capital: Results from a Field Experiment," ScienceDirect 36, no. 3 (September 2007): 1156–1183, https://www.sciencedirect.com/science/article/pii/S0049089X06000767.

15 Whitney Johnson, "Are You Stuck in a Girls' Club?" *Harvard Business Review,* December 27, 2011, https://hbr.org/2011/12/are-you-stuck-in-a-girls-club.

16 Gina Belli, "How Many Jobs Are Found Through Networking, Really?" PayScale, April 6, 2017, https://www.payscale.com/career-news/2017/04/many-jobs-found-networking.

17 Barbara Kiviat, "Why Personal Connections Matter and Can Get You Hired," Glassdoor, October 25, 2013, https://www.glassdoor.com/blog/personal-connections-matter-hired.

18 Brian Uzzi, "Research: Men and Women Need Different Kinds of Networks to Succeed," *Harvard Business Review,* February 25, 2019, https://hbr.org/2019/02/research-men-and-women-need-different-kinds-of-networks-to-succeed.

19 Christine Silva, "The Myth of the Ideal Worker: Does Doing All the Right Things Really Get Women Ahead?," Catalyst, October 1, 2011, https://www.catalyst.org/research/the-myth-of-the-ideal-worker-does-doing-all-the-right-things-really-get-women-ahead/.

20 Shelley J. Correll and Lori Nishiura Mackenzie, "To Succeed in Tech, Women Need More Visibility," *Harvard Business Review*, September 13, 2016, https://hbr.org/2016/09/to-succeed-in-tech-women-need-more-visibility.

21 "Risk, Resilience, Reward: Mastering the Three 'R's': The Key to. Women's Success in the Workspace," KPMG, 2019, https://info.kpmg.us/content/dam/info/en/news-perspectives/pdf/2019/KPMG_Womens_Leadership_Study.pdf.

22 Priya Fielding-Singh, Devon Magliozzi, and Swethaa Ballakrishnen, "Why Women Stay Out of the Spotlight at Work," *Harvard Business Review*, August 28, 2018, https://hbr.org/2018/08/why-women-stay-out-of-the-spotlight-at-work.

23 "KPMG Women's Leadership Study: Moving Women Forward into Leadership Roles," KPMG, 2015, https://home.kpmg/content/dam/kpmg/ph/pdf/ThoughtLeadershipPublications/KPMGWomensLeadershipStudy.pdf.

24 Dan Ariely, "The Significant Objects Project," danariely.com, December 25, 2009, https://danariely.com/the-significant-objects-project/.

25 "KPMG Women's Leadership Study: Moving
    Women Forward into Leadership Roles,"
    KPMG, 2015, https://home.kpmg/content/dam/
    kpmg/ph/pdf/ThoughtLeadershipPublications/
    KPMGWomensLeadershipStudy.pdf.

26 Amy Cuddy, "Your Body Language May Shape
    Who You Are," filmed October 1, 2012, video, 20:25,
    https://www.ted.com/talks/amy_cuddy_your_body_
    language_may_shape_who_you_are.

27 "7 38 55 Rule of Communication,"
    toolshero, 2012, https://www.toolshero.com/
    communication-skills/7-38-55-rule.

28 Elena Doldor, Madeleine Wyatt, and Jo Silvester,
    "Research: Men Get More Actionable Feedback Than
    Women," *Harvard Business Review,* February 10,
    2021, https://hbr.org/2021/02/research-men-get-
    more-actionable-feedback-than-women.

29 "The Rise in Dual Income Households," *Pew Research
    Center,* June 18, 2015, https://www.pewresearch.org/
    ft_dual-income-households-1960-2012-2/.

30 Jennifer Garcia-Alonso, Matt Krentz, Deborah Lovich, and Stuart Quickenden, "Lightening the Mental Load That Holds Women Back," BCG, April 10, 2019, https://www.bcg.com/publications/2019/lightening-mental-load-holds-women-back.

31 "Lightening the Mental Load," Diversity Woman Media, May 8, 2021, https://www.diversitywoman.com/lightening-the-mental-load.

32 Dina Gerdeman, "Kids of Working Moms Grow into Happy Adults," Harvard Business School, July 16, 2018, https://hbswk.hbs.edu/item/kids-of-working-moms-grow-into-happy-adults.

33 Andrea Caumont and Wendy Wang, "5 Questions (and Answers) About American Moms Today," *Pew Research Center*, May 9, 2014, https://www.pewresearch.org/fact-tank/2014/05/09/5-questions-and-answers-about-american-moms-today/.

34 Allison Preiss, "New CAP Calculator Reveals the Hidden, Lifetime Costs of the Child Care Crisis in the US," Center for American Progress, June 21, 2016, https://www.americanprogress.org/press/release/2016/06/21/139014/release-new-cap-calculator-reveals-the-hidden-lifetime-costs-of-the-child-care-crisis-in-the-u-s.

35 Bill Pelster, Jennifer Stempel, and Bernard van der Vyver, "Careers and Learning: Real Time, All the Time," Deloitte, February 28, 2017, https://www2. deloitte.com/us/en/insights/focus/human-capital-trends/2017/learning-in-the-digital-age.html.

36 Allison Preiss, "New CAP Calculator Reveals the Hidden, Lifetime Cost of the Child Care Crisis in the US," Center for American Progress, June 21, 2016, https://www.americanprogress.org/press/ release/2016/06/21/139014/release-new-cap-calculator-reveals-the-hidden-lifetime-costs-of-the-child-care-crisis-in-the-u-s/.

37 Roger Trapp, "Women Aiming for Top Jobs 'Must Take Control of Their Own Careers,'" *Forbes*, January 29, 2018, https://www.forbes.com/ sites/rogertrapp/2018/01/29/women-aiming-for-top-jobs-must-take-control-of-their-own-careers/#21d87f3f6292.

38 Avivah Wittenberg-Cox, "If You Can't Find a Spouse Who Supports Your Career, Stay Single," *Harvard Business Review,* October 24, 2017, https:// hbr.org/2017/10/if-you-cant-find-a-spouse-who-supports-your-career-stay-single.

39 Drew Weisholtz, "Women Do 2 More Hours of Housework Daily than Men, Study Says," *Today*, January 22, 2020, https://www.today.com/news/women-do-2-more-hours-housework-daily-men-study-says-t172272.

40 Claire Cain Miller, "Young Men Embrace Gender Equality, But They Still Don't Vacuum," *The New York Times*, February 11, 2020, https://www.nytimes.com/2020/02/11/upshot/gender-roles-housework.html.

41 Claire Cain Miller, "Millennial Men Aren't the Dads They Thought They'd Be," *The New York Times*, July 30, 2015, https://www.nytimes.com/2015/07/31/upshot/millennial-men-find-work-and-family-hard-to-balance.html.

42 Barbara Annis, Carolyn Lawrence, and Patsy Doerr, "Solutions to Women's Advancement," *Women of Influence*, http://www.womenofinfluence.ca/wp-content/uploads/2014/04/Women-of-Influence-WhitePaper-2014.pdf.

43 Sarah Coury et al., "Women in the Workplace," McKinsey & Company, September 30, 2020, https://www.mckinsey.com/featured-insights/diversity-and-inclusion/women-in-the-workplace.

44 Elise Gould, Jessica Schieder, and Kathleen Geier, "What Is the Gender Pay Gap and Is It Real?", *Economic Policy Institute,* October 20, 2016, https://www.epi.org/publication/what-is-the-gender-pay-gap-and-is-it-real/#epi-toc-13.

45 "Women's Earnings: The Pay Gap (Quick Take)," Catalyst, March 23, 2021, https://www.catalyst.org/research/womens-earnings-the-pay-gap/.

46 Shelley J. Correll, Stephen Bernard, and In Paik, "Getting a Job: Is There a Motherhood Penalty?" *American Journal of Sociology* 112, No. 5 (March 2007): 1297–1339, https://sociology.stanford.edu/sites/g/files/sbiybj9501/f/publications/getting_a_job-_is_there_a_motherhood_penalty.pdf.

47 Michelle Fox, "The 'Motherhood Penalty' Is Real, and It Costs Women $16,000 a Year in Lost Wages," *CNBC,* March 25, 2019, https://www.cnbc.com/2019/03/25/the-motherhood-penalty-costs-women-16000-a-year-in-lost-wages.html.